THE NERVOUS SYSTEM

THE ENCYCLOPEDIA OF

H E A L T H

THE HEALTHY BODY

Dale C. Garell, M.D. • General Editor

THE NERVOUS SYSTEM

Edward Edelson

Introduction by C. Everett Koop, M.D., Sc.D.
former Surgeon General, U.S. Public Health Service

CHELSEA HOUSE PUBLISHERS

New York • Philadelphia

The goal of the ENCYCLOPEDIA OF HEALTH *is to provide general information in the ever-changing areas of physiology, psychology, and related medical issues. The titles in this series are not intended to take the place of the professional advice of a physician or other health care professional.*

ON THE COVER: Colorized scanning electron micrograph of neurons from the cerebral cortex, magnified 162 times.

Chelsea House Publishers
EDITOR-IN-CHIEF   Remmel Nunn
MANAGING EDITOR   Karyn Gullen Browne
COPY CHIEF   Juliann Barbato
PICTURE EDITOR   Adrian G. Allen
ART DIRECTOR   Maria Epes
DEPUTY COPY CHIEF   Mark Rifkin
ASSISTANT ART DIRECTOR   Noreen Romano
MANUFACTURING MANAGER   Gerald Levine
SYSTEMS MANAGER   Lindsey Ottman
PRODUCTION MANAGER   Joseph Romano
PRODUCTION COORDINATOR   Marie Claire Cebrián

The Encyclopedia of Health
SENIOR EDITOR   Brian Feinberg

Staff for THE NERVOUS SYSTEM
ASSISTANT EDITOR   Leigh Hope Wood
COPY EDITOR   Brian Sookram
EDITORIAL ASSISTANT   Bouqui Kya-Hill
PICTURE RESEARCHER   Georganne Backman
SENIOR DESIGNER   Marjorie Zaum

5   7   9   8   6   4

Library of Congress Cataloging-in-Publication Data

Edelson, Edward
    I. The Nervous system/by Ed Edelson
        p.   cm.—(The Encyclopedia of health)
    Includes bibliographical references (p. 93).
    Summary: Discusses the nervous system and its components and how they function.
    ISBN 0-7910-0023-0
        0-7910-0464-3 (pbk.)
    1. Nervous system—Physiology—Juvenile literature. 2. Nervous system—
Diseases—Juvenile literature. [1. Nervous system] I. Title. II. Series.   90-1723
QP361.5.E34 1990   CIP
612.8—dc20   AC

CONTENTS

THE ENCYCLOPEDIA OF
H E A L T H

THE HEALTHY BODY

The Circulatory System
Dental Health
The Digestive System
The Endocrine System
Exercise
Genetics & Heredity
The Human Body: An Overview
Hygiene
The Immune System
Memory & Learning
The Musculoskeletal System
The Nervous System
Nutrition
The Reproductive System
The Respiratory System
The Senses
Speech & Hearing
Sports Medicine
Vision
Vitamins & Minerals

THE LIFE CYCLE

Adolescence
Adulthood
Aging
Childhood
Death & Dying
The Family
Friendship & Love
Pregnancy & Birth

MEDICAL ISSUES

Careers in Health Care
Environmental Health
Folk Medicine
Health Care Delivery
Holistic Medicine
Medical Ethics
Medical Fakes & Frauds
Medical Technology
Medicine & the Law
Occupational Health
Public Health

PYSCHOLOGICAL DISORDERS AND THEIR TREATMENT

Anxiety & Phobias
Child Abuse
Compulsive Behavior
Delinquency & Criminal Behavior
Depression
Diagnosing & Treating Mental Illness
Eating Habits & Disorders
Learning Disabilities
Mental Retardation
Personality Disorders
Schizophrenia
Stress Management
Suicide

MEDICAL DISORDERS AND THEIR TREATMENT

AIDS
Allergies
Alzheimer's Disease
Arthritis
Birth Defects
Cancer
The Common Cold
Diabetes
Emergency Medicine
Gynecological Disorders
Headaches
The Hospital
Kidney Disorders
Medical Diagnosis
The Mind-Body Connection
Mononucleosis and Other Infectious Diseases
Nuclear Medicine
Organ Transplants
Pain
Physical Handicaps
Poisons & Toxins
Prescription & OTC Drugs
Sexually Transmitted Diseases
Skin Disorders
Stroke & Heart Disease
Substance Abuse
Tropical Medicine

PREVENTION AND EDUCATION: THE KEYS TO GOOD HEALTH

C. Everett Koop, M.D., Sc.D.
former Surgeon General,
U.S. Public Health Service

The issue of health education has received particular attention in recent years because of the presence of AIDS in the news. But our response to this particular tragedy points up a number of broader issues that doctors, public health officials, educators, and the public face. In particular, it points up the necessity for sound health education for citizens of all ages.

Over the past 25 years this country has been able to bring about dramatic declines in the death rates for heart disease, stroke, accidents, and for people under the age of 45, cancer. Today, Americans generally eat better and take better care of themselves than ever before. Thus, with the help of modern science and technology, they have a better chance of surviving serious—even catastrophic—illnesses. That's the good news.

But, like every phonograph record, there's a flip side, and one with special significance for young adults. According to a report issued in 1979 by Dr. Julius Richmond, my predecessor as Surgeon General, Americans aged 15 to 24 had a higher death rate in 1979 than they did 20 years earlier. The causes: violent death and injury, alcohol and drug abuse, unwanted pregnancies, and sexually transmitted diseases. Adolescents are particularly vulnerable because they are beginning to explore their own sexuality and perhaps to experiment with drugs. The need for educating young people is critical, and the price of neglect is high.

Yet even for the population as a whole, our health is still far from what it could be. Why? A 1974 Canadian government report attributed all death and disease to four broad elements: inadequacies in the health care system, behavioral factors or unhealthy life-styles, environmental hazards, and human biological factors.

To be sure, there are diseases that are still beyond the control of even our advanced medical knowledge and techniques. And despite yearnings that are as old as the human race itself, there is no "fountain of youth" to ward off aging and death. Still, there is a solution to many of the problems that undermine sound health. In a word, that solution is prevention. Prevention, which includes health promotion and education, saves lives, improves the quality of life, and in the long run, saves money.

In the United States, organized public health activities and preventive medicine have a long history. Important milestones in this country or foreign breakthroughs adopted in the United States include the improvement of sanitary procedures and the development of pasteurized milk in the late 19th century and the introduction in the mid-20th century of effective vaccines against polio, measles, German measles, mumps, and other once-rampant diseases. Internationally, organized public health efforts began on a wide-scale basis with the International Sanitary Conference of 1851, to which 12 nations sent representatives. The World Health Organization, founded in 1948, continues these efforts under the aegis of the United Nations, with particular emphasis on combating communicable diseases and the training of health care workers.

Despite these accomplishments, much remains to be done in the field of prevention. For too long, we have had a medical care system that is science- and technology-based, focused, essentially, on illness and mortality. It is now patently obvious that both the social and the economic costs of such a system are becoming insupportable.

Implementing prevention—and its corollaries, health education and promotion—is the job of several groups of people.

First, the medical and scientific professions need to continue basic scientific research, and here we are making considerable progress. But increased concern with prevention will also have a decided impact on how primary care doctors practice medicine. With a shift to health-based rather than morbidity-based medicine, the role of the "new physician" will include a healthy dose of patient education.

Second, practitioners of the social and behavioral sciences—psychologists, economists, city planners—along with lawyers, business leaders, and government officials—must solve the practical and ethical dilemmas confronting us: poverty, crime, civil rights, literacy, education, employment, housing, sanitation, environmental protection, health care delivery systems, and so forth. All of these issues affect public health.

Third is the public at large. We'll consider that very important group in a moment.

Fourth, and the linchpin in this effort, is the public health profession—doctors, epidemiologists, teachers—who must harness the professional expertise of the first two groups and the common sense and cooperation of the third, the public. They must define the problems statistically and qualitatively and then help us set priorities for finding the solutions.

To a very large extent, improving those statistics is the responsibility of every individual. So let's consider more specifically what the role of the individual should be and why health education is so important to that role. First, and most obvious, individuals can protect themselves from illness and injury and thus minimize their need for professional medical care. They can eat nutritious food, get adequate exercise, avoid tobacco, alcohol, and drugs, and take prudent steps to avoid accidents. The proverbial "apple a day keeps the doctor away" is not so far from the truth, after all.

Second, individuals should actively participate in their own medical care. They should schedule regular medical and dental checkups. Should they develop an illness or injury, they should know when to treat themselves and when to seek professional help. To gain the maximum benefit from any medical treatment that they do require, individuals must become partners in that treatment. For instance, they should understand the effects and side effects of medications. I counsel young physicians that there is no such thing as too much information when talking with patients. But the corollary is the patient must know enough about the nuts and bolts of the healing process to understand what the doctor is telling him or her. That is at least partially the patient's responsibility.

Education is equally necessary for us to understand the ethical and public policy issues in health care today. Sometimes individuals will encounter these issues in making decisions about their own treatment or that of family members. Other citizens may encounter them as jurors in medical malpractice cases. But we all become involved, indirectly, when we elect our public officials, from school board members to the president. Should surrogate parenting be legal? To what extent is drug testing desirable, legal, or necessary? Should there be public funding for family planning, hospitals, various types of medical research, and other medical care for the indigent? How should we allocate scant technological resources, such as kidney dialysis and organ transplants? What is the proper role of government in protecting the rights of patients?

What are the broad goals of public health in the United States today? In 1980, the Public Health Service issued a report aptly entitled *Promoting Health—Preventing Disease: Objectives for the Nation.* This report expressed its goals in terms of mortality and in terms of intermediate goals in education and health improvement. It identified 15 major concerns: controlling high blood pressure; improving family planning; improving pregnancy care and infant health; increasing the rate of immunization; controlling sexually transmitted diseases; controlling the presence of toxic agents and radiation in the environment; improving occupational safety and health; preventing accidents; promoting water fluoridation and dental health; controlling infectious diseases; decreasing smoking; decreasing alcohol and drug abuse; improving nutrition; promoting physical fitness and exercise; and controlling stress and violent behavior.

For healthy adolescents and young adults (ages 15 to 24), the specific goal was a 20% reduction in deaths, with a special focus on motor vehicle injuries and alcohol and drug abuse. For adults (ages 25 to 64), the aim was 25% fewer deaths, with a concentration on heart attacks, strokes, and cancers.

Smoking is perhaps the best example of how individual behavior can have a direct impact on health. Today, cigarette smoking is recognized as the single most important preventable cause of death in our society. It is responsible for more cancers and more cancer deaths than any other known agent; is a prime risk factor for heart and blood vessel disease, chronic bronchitis, and emphysema; and is a frequent cause of complications in pregnancies and of babies born prematurely, underweight, or with potentially fatal respiratory and cardiovascular problems.

Since the release of the Surgeon General's first report on smoking in 1964, the proportion of adult smokers has declined substantially, from 43% in 1965 to 30.5% in 1985. Since 1965, 37 million people have quit smoking. Although there is still much work to be done if we are to become a "smoke-free society," it is heartening to note that public health and public education efforts—such as warnings on cigarette packages and bans on broadcast advertising—have already had significant effects.

In 1835, Alexis de Tocqueville, a French visitor to America, wrote, "In America the passion for physical well-being is general." Today, as then, health and fitness are front-page items. But with the greater scientific and technological resources now available to us, we are in a far stronger position to make good health care available to everyone. And with the greater technological threats to us as we approach the 21st century, the need to do so is more urgent than ever before. Comprehensive information about basic biology, preventive medicine, medical and surgical treatments, and related ethical and public policy issues can help you arm yourself with the knowledge you need to be healthy throughout your life.

FOREWORD

Dale C. Garell, M.D.

Advances in our understanding of health and disease during the 20th century have been truly remarkable. Indeed, it could be argued that modern health care is one of the greatest accomplishments in all of human history. In the early 20th century, improvements in sanitation, water treatment, and sewage disposal reduced death rates and increased longevity. Previously untreatable illnesses can now be managed with antibiotics, immunizations, and modern surgical techniques. Discoveries in the fields of immunology, genetic diagnosis, and organ transplantation are revolutionizing the prevention and treatment of disease. Modern medicine is even making inroads against cancer and heart disease, two of the leading causes of death in the United States.

Although there is much to be proud of, medicine continues to face enormous challenges. Science has vanquished diseases such as smallpox and polio, but new killers, most notably AIDS, confront us. Moreover, we now victimize ourselves with what some have called "diseases of choice," or those brought on by drug and alcohol abuse, bad eating habits, and mismanagement of the stresses and strains of contemporary life. The very technology that is doing so much to prolong life has brought with it previously unimaginable ethical dilemmas related to issues of death and dying. The rising cost of health care is a matter of central concern to us all. And violence in the form of automobile accidents, homicide, and suicide remains the major killer of young adults.

In the past, most people were content to leave health care and medical treatment in the hands of professionals. But since the 1960s, the consumer of medical care—that is, the patient—has assumed an increasingly central role in the management of his or her own health. There has also been a new emphasis placed on prevention: People are recognizing that their own actions can help prevent many of the conditions that have caused death and disease in the past. This accounts for the growing commitment to good nutrition and regular exercise, for the increasing number of people who are choosing not to smoke, and for a new moderation in people's drinking habits.

People want to know more about themselves and their own health. They are curious about their body: its anatomy, physiology, and biochemistry. They want to keep up with rapidly evolving medical technologies and procedures. They are willing to educate themselves about common disorders and diseases so that they can be full partners in their own health care.

THE ENCYCLOPEDIA OF HEALTH is designed to provide the basic knowledge that readers will need if they are to take significant responsibility for their own health. It is also meant to serve as a frame of reference for further study and exploration. The encyclopedia is divided into five subsections: The Healthy Body; The Life Cycle; Medical Disorders and Their Treatment; Psychological Disorders and Their Treatment; and Medical Issues. For each topic covered by the encyclopedia, we present the essential facts about the relevant biology; the symptoms, diagnosis, and treatment of common diseases and disorders; and ways in which you can prevent or reduce the severity of health problems when that is possible. The encyclopedia also projects what may lie ahead in the way of future treatment or prevention strategies.

The broad range of topics and issues covered in the encyclopedia reflects that human health encompasses physical, psychological, social, environmental, and spiritual well-being. Just as the mind and the body are inextricably linked, so, too, is the individual an integral part of the wider world that comprises his or her family, society, and environment. To discuss health in its broadest aspect it is necessary to explore the many ways in which it is connected to such fields as law, social science, public policy, economics, and even religion. And so, the encyclopedia is meant to be a bridge between science, medical technology, the world at large, and you. I hope that it will inspire you to pursue in greater depth particular areas of interest and that you will take advantage of the suggestions for further reading and the lists of resources and organizations that can provide additional information.

CHAPTER 1

THE NEURON

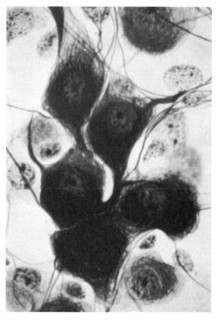

A microphotograph of nerve cells

French philosopher René Descartes said "I think, therefore I am." In making that statement, he indirectly paid tribute to the importance of the human nervous system, a wondrous network that is not only the engine of thought but the driving force that controls the entire body. *Neurons* (nerve cells) are the basic units of this network, and all of the activities of the nervous system, from a simple reflex to a complex human thought, are accomplished by these highly specialized cells.

Though the nervous system of a human being is far more advanced than that of much simpler animals, such as the squid or frog, the neurons of all creatures are essentially identical. Indeed, most of what scientists know about the way neurons work has been learned from experiments using nerve cells from lower animals and applying that information to people.

THE STRUCTURE OF THE NEURON

The neuron is a remarkably complex cell that even today is only partially understood. The nerve cell was first viewed by Italian physician Camillo Golgi, who in 1873 developed a way to stain neurons, chemically darkening them so that their finer details stood out under a microscope.

Golgi's stained samples of nervous tissue showed a web of neurons, individual nerve cells that came close to each other but never quite

With an improved version of the Italian physician Camillo Golgi's (ca. 1844–1926) stain, Spanish scientist Santiago Ramón y Cajal (1852–1934), shown here, proved that the entire nervous system is composed of individual nerve cells, or neurons.

touched. Golgi's work led a German anatomist, Wilhelm Waldeyer, to propose—correctly—that the entire nervous system was composed of neurons.

That contention was proved by the Spanish scientist Santiago Ramón y Cajal, one of the great figures in neurological research. During the late 19th century, using an improved version of Golgi's stain, Ramón y Cajal was able to work out the complex connections of neurons in the brain and spinal cord.

A Cell Like No Other

Although it contains a nucleus and other parts common to cells, the neuron is unusual because, in complex animals, it ceases to divide, or reproduce, after a certain point. In humans and other mammals, that point is reached at birth. Although connections among neurons are formed throughout life in these animals, no new nerve cells are produced.

Neurons are also different from other cells because of their well-developed ability to send messages through a combination of electrical and chemical means. The nerve cell is able to do so because of its specialized structures. Sprouting from the cell body are stringlike processes called *dendrites* and one long, relatively thick extension called the *axon*. These two structures, which are also known as *nerve fibers*, give the neuron a unique look. They led Ramón y Cajal to describe the nerve cell as "the aristocrat among the structures of the body, with its giant arms stretched out like the tentacles of an octopus to the provinces on the frontier of the outside world, to watch for the constant ambushes of physical and chemical forces."

Though some special kinds of neurons do not have dendrites, most have at least one, and many have several. Any of these dendrites can make contact with a number of other nerve cells. The dendrites receive signals from neighboring neurons and conduct these signals back to their own cell, whereas the axon conducts the impulses away from the neuron to other nerve cells.

The axon can run up to several feet in length and contains a number of branches that allow it to make connections with many other cells as

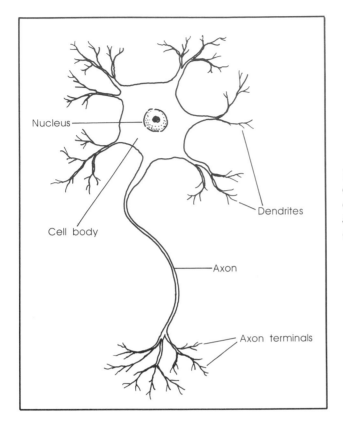

Nucleus

Cell body

Dendrites

Axon

Axon terminals

The neuron uses its axon and dendrites to conduct electrochemical signals to and from other neurons.

well. The point at which it makes contact, the space between the axon and its target cell, is a gap called the *synapse*, across which one neuron transmits information to another.

ELECTRICAL PROPERTIES OF THE NEURON

Nerve action was first discovered to be associated with electricity in the 1780s by the Italian anatomist Luigi Galvani, who showed that an electrical charge made muscles contract. In one of his experiments, Galvani attached a lightning rod to a severed frog leg, stretched a wire from the leg to water, and waited for an oncoming thunderstorm. When lightning flashed, electrical impulses carried by the frog's neurons caused its muscles to contract frequently and intensely.

In the late 19th century, the German chemist and physicist Walther Hermann Nernst proposed that the electrical activity of the neuron results from the passage of *ions*, or electrically charged atoms, through the cell's outer membrane.

Finally, in the early 1950s, British scientists Alan Lloyd Hodgkin and Andrew Fielding Huxley, through experiments using the giant axon of the squid, were able to work out the step-by-step sequence leading to the conduction of an electrical impulse from a neuron.

The Electrical Impulse

Ions are found in the fluids that bathe the body's cells. Chief among these atoms are potassium and sodium ions, which are equally and positively charged. The membrane of a neuron, like that of other cells, contains many holes called *ion channels,* which allow specific kinds of ions to pass in and out. Some channels, for example, will only let potassium ions through, whereas others can only be crossed by sodium ions. In addition, some of the channels for these ions have "gates" that control when an ion can go in or out; other channels are always open. Most potassium channels do not have gates, thus potassium ions can freely pass through the membrane at any time; most sodium channels have gates that are open on some occasions and closed on others.

When at rest, a neuron contains a high concentration of potassium ions and a low concentration of sodium ions compared to the fluid that surrounds and bathes it, thanks to a mechanism that pumps sodium out of the cell and potassium into it. Even though both potassium and sodium ions are positively charged, the neuron has a negative charge relative to the fluid outside it because the nerve cell also contains negatively charged protein molecules. Because of their large size, these protein molecules are unable to pass through any ion channel in the membrane and so are trapped inside the neuron.

When a nerve cell is stimulated (say, by plunging one's hand into a tub of warm water), sodium channels open suddenly. Sodium pours in, partially because of the electrical attraction of the positive sodium to the cell's negative charge. The inside of the cell then becomes positively charged, which, as a result, sends an electrical impulse sweeping down the axon until this signal reaches the synapse.

Once the neuron has "fired" (sent out an electrical impulse), the normal balance of ions is restored and the cell stops discharging electricity. Of course, the sensations people feel often last much longer than the split second of an impulse "firing." For example, the hand soaking in a tub of warm water will continue to feel warm until it is lifted out again, because the nerve cells continue their cycle again and again: firing an impulse, restoring their normal ion balance, charging up again, firing another impulse, and so on.

To describe these events, scientists use the language of physics. When the ion balance is normal, and the neuron is not being charged, the resting nerve cell is said to be *polarized* and to have a *resting potential*—the negative charge relative to the outside of the cell. When the neuron gears up to fire, the membrane *depolarizes*; the electrical impulse then sent is called the *action potential*.

The speed with which an impulse travels down a human nerve fiber depends in part on the diameter of the fiber: The larger the diameter, the faster the impulse. The thinnest fibers conduct impulses at a speed of about 40 inches per second, or roughly 2 miles per hour. The thickest fibers conduct about 100 times faster. The speed of the impulse also depends on whether the fiber is insulated. On some nerve cells, a fatty substance called *myelin* forms an insulating sheath around the axon. This allows the neuron to conduct an electrical impulse more efficiently and, therefore, more quickly. When the myelin sheath is damaged, as in the disease called *multiple sclerosis*, nerve cell function is severely impaired.

Whatever the speed of the impulse, its magnitude is always the same. A strong stimulus (such as stepping on a tack barefoot) can make a nerve cell fire more frequently, but it does not make each firing stronger. However, the strength of the stimulus determines whether a nerve cell does or does not fire. When the stimulation is strong enough, the neuron's membrane reaches what is called its *threshold potential* and the nerve cell fires. The changes that cause it to fire are called the *all-or-none response* because they either occur or do not occur depending on the strength of the stimulus.

The instrument used in experiments performed by Luigi Galvani (1737–98), who discovered that electricity causes muscles to contract

Chemical Transmission

Running down the axon, the electrical impulse reaches the synapse. For a long time, there was a vigorous debate about how the nerve cell transmitted information across this gap. However, even before the electrical nature of the neuron was clarified, the transmission debate was settled. In 1921, German physiologist Otto Loewi determined that a chemical called *acetylcholine* transmitted signals across the synapse from one nerve cell to another. As it turns out, acetylcholine is only one of many such signal-transmitting substances, now called *neurotransmitters*.

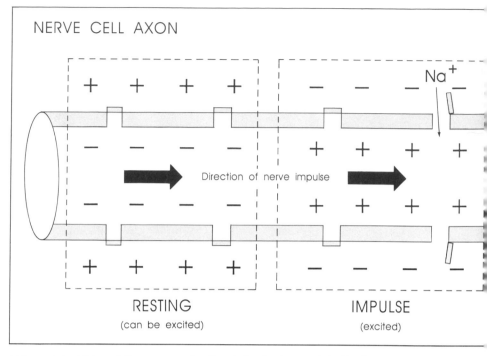

NERVE CELL AXON

Na$^+$

Direction of nerve impulse

RESTING
(can be excited)

IMPULSE
(excited)

When a section of the neuron is stimulated, channels in that area open and sodium ions pour into the cell. The inside of the cell at that point becomes positively charged, and this signal then moves through the neuron.

When an electrical impulse reaches the synapse, neurotransmitter molecules are released from the end of the axon; they then cross the gap and act on the adjacent neuron. These molecules may activate that neuron so that the electrical signal continues its journey. In other cases, however, the impulses "tell" the nerve cell not to pass them to another neuron. (Some portions of the brain, for example, have to be prevented from transmitting messages so that information can be routed through better brain pathways.) The neurotransmitters are then either reabsorbed by the neuron that released them or swept away by what are called scavenger molecules.

Research in recent years has revived the idea that, in rare cases, signals can be transmitted from nerve to nerve by electrical impulse alone, with no help from neurotransmitter chemicals. It is true that

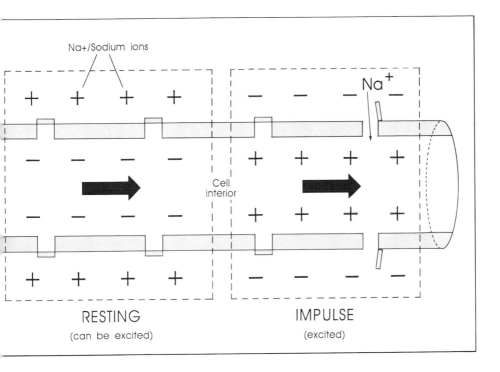

Na+/Sodium ions

Cell interior

RESTING
(can be excited)

IMPULSE
(excited)

neurotransmitters do the job at most synapses, but there are some places in the nervous system where electrical signals jump directly from neuron to neuron. This kind of transmission may exist where a speedy response is of the essence.

THE ORGANIZATION OF NEURONS

It is rare for a nerve cell to make contact with only one other neuron. As mentioned, a neuron usually sends out its axon to form connections with many other cells. In addition, an average-sized neuron in the spinal cord has hundreds of dendrites; thus it can simultaneously receive hundreds of signals from other neurons, some activating the nerve cell so that it will pick up and send an electrical impulse from other neurons, and some preventing it from passing on signals. This sort of complex interaction goes on constantly.

Neurons are found in groups, with their axons bunched together like stalks. In the *central nervous system*—the brain and spinal cord—these bundles of axons are whitish in color and so are called *white matter*. The main part of each cell, the *cell body*, where the nucleus resides, is grayish in color; thus a mass of cell bodies is called *gray matter*. In the *peripheral nervous system*—the network of neurons outside the central nervous system—collections of cell bodies are called *ganglia*, and bundles of axons are called *neurons* (as opposed to nerve cells, which consist of the cell bodies and axons together).

Supporting Cells

Neurons do not act in isolation. They almost invariably come with companion cells, called *neuroglia*, that help them function. In the central nervous system, there are four kinds of neuroglia: *astrocytes*, *ependymal cells*, *microglia*, and *oligodendrocytes*, each type offering some sort of protection for the neurons, from fighting infection to forming a barrier against harmful substances in the bloodstream. Each has its own unique structure and function. In the peripheral nervous system, there is only one kind of neuroglial cell, the Schwann cell, named after German physiologist Theodor Schwann. Schwann cells not only manufacture myelin but also appear to play an important role in the repair of nervous tissue. This function dramatically distinguishes the neurons of the peripheral nervous system from those in the brain and spinal cord: When a neuron in the spinal cord is severely injured or cut, it does not regenerate (this subject will be further discussed in Chapter 7). Neurons in the peripheral nervous system do regenerate.

CHAPTER 2

THE CENTRAL NERVOUS SYSTEM

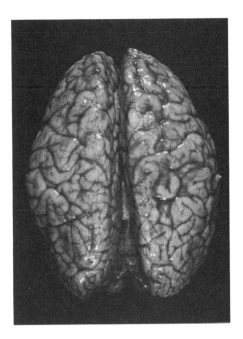

A view of the human brain from above, showing the longitudinal sulcus and the many sulci of the cortex

The brain is perhaps the most remarkable organ in the body. It not only controls human thought and emotions but also integrates all the body's internal activities and oversees all contact with the outside world. The 100 billion neurons in the brain are the essence of this extraordinary organ, with each nerve cell having as many as 1,000 connections, or synapses, that allow the brain to receive and transmit complex messages.

This maze of links within the brain enables the nervous system to perform its tasks, so scientists have begun to focus on these connections in order to better understand how the brain functions. Some researchers are studying early brain development, when the first neural hookups are made.

NEURAL DEVELOPMENT

The development of a human being starts as soon as a sperm cell penetrates an egg. The fertilized egg begins to divide into a ball of cells, and as these cells develop, each becomes distinct and specialized. One may become part of a bone or a muscle, and another may become part of the brain.

After approximately two weeks, the ball has flattened and the cells have formed three distinct layers: the *ectoderm*, *mesoderm*, and *endoderm*. Out of the ectoderm, both the brain and the spinal cord will develop.

A sheet of cells called the *neural plate* forms within the ectodermal layer, and neurons begin to develop within this sheet. The neural plate then folds over on itself to form the *neural tube*, from which the nervous system will develop. Just after the tube forms, neurons begin to multiply at a faster rate. Over a period of time, groups of neurons stop dividing and migrate to their destined areas in the nervous system, where they continue to grow and mature. At this point in development, the first neural connections are made.

As the neurons grow, axons begin to bud from them. At the tip of every growing axon is a structure called the *growth cone*, which was discovered by Ramón y Cajal in the late 19th century. This cone sends out many thin projections called *filopodia*, and these fasten to a target area, pulling the axon toward its proper connection, such as another nerve cell in the network.

How the growth cone finds its target in the first place, however, is a mystery. Roger Sperry of the California Institute of Technology, whose brain research netted him a 1981 Nobel Prize, developed the general theory that certain nerve cell connections common to all humans are made because of chemical attractions between a growing axon and its target. Many experiments have, in fact, supported this argument.

One version of this theory suggests that surface molecules guide the growth of the axon. The surface molecules, each specific for a certain pathway, are recognized only by receptor molecules on target neurons. Though many types of growth-regulating molecules have been discovered, much remains to be learned.

THE BRAIN

One of the critical operations in brain development is the formation of detailed connections with the rest of the body, such as the link between the *retina* (the back portion of the eye that catches images) and the region of the brain concerned with vision. Psychologist Roger Sperry discovered much of what is now known about this process. Essentially, the pattern of connections to the brain must be exactly the same as the pattern of neurons in the retina, so that the image seen by the eye is

Roger Sperry played an important role in determining how connections between neurons are made.

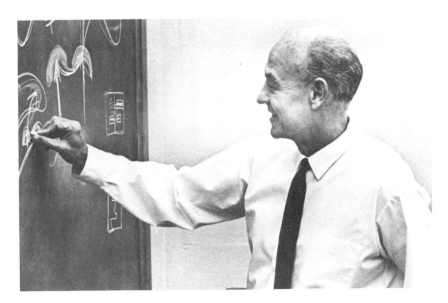

reproduced point by point in the brain. The development of this parallel structure is accomplished through chemical guidance.

Electrical stimulation and cell death appear to help fine-tune connections between the retina and the brain: The neurons grow from the retina toward the brain; once they have established the correct connections, the circuits are strengthened as electrical impulses begin to carry signals from the eye to the brain. Small errors in connections are corrected by gradual shifts in the location of an axon, although if an error is too large to correct, the neuron dies.

Before birth, in its first month, the human embryo has a nervous system no more advanced than that of a worm. Within five months, all the structures of the brain have formed. The three primary structures are the *forebrain*, *midbrain*, and *hindbrain*.

Throughout its 9 months of prenatal development, the human brain produces 250,000 neurons every minute, although half of these die by the time of birth—at least some, as mentioned, as a result of faulty connections with other nerve cells. Though neurons are no longer formed once a child is born, support cells continue to grow for up to a year after birth. Moreover, many subtle connections continue to be made within the prominent structures of the brain. Thus, although the brain of a newborn may be one-fourth the weight of an adult brain, within six months it can reach half of its adult weight.

From one kind of vertebrate to another, from fish to humans, the hindbrain, midbrain, and forebrain differ in size and capacity to handle various functions. It is important to remember, however, that size alone is no indication of how advanced a brain is. The brain of a dolphin, horse, elephant, or ape clearly outweighs that of a human. Yet humans are at the top of the evolutionary ladder because the *cerebrum* of the human brain is more developed than that of any other animal.

The Forebrain

The forebrain, the cerebrum in particular, distinguishes humans from all other animals. In fish, the cerebrum is a rather small swelling concerned primarily with the sense of smell. In advanced animals, namely primates such as monkeys, apes, and humans, the cerebrum is much larger and more complex.

The human cerebrum is the top portion of the brain; it is divided by a deep crevice, called the *longitudinal sulcus*, which separates it into left and right *cerebral hemispheres*. Although these look identical, there is a division of labor, with each hemisphere controlling the *motor* (movement) and *sensory* (taste, touch, vision, smell, and hearing) functions of the other side of the body. Nerve fibers from the left side of the body go to the right side of the brain and vice versa.

The hemispheres are covered by a layer of gray matter called the *cortex* and have a layer of white matter underneath. The surface of the cortex looks wrinkled, with a multitude of ridges, called *gyri*, and furrows, called *sulci*. These serve to increase the size of the surface layer so that there are many more neurons in the cortex than there would be without the wrinkles. The sheet of gray matter is only a fraction of an inch thick but is so ingeniously convoluted that it has an area of 400 square inches and accounts for more than a third of the weight of the brain. However, about 80% of the cortex has no clearly identifiable function. Scientists presume that neurons in this portion of the brain engage in general data processing that helps the specialized centers of the brain to function.

The traditional anatomical approach divides each of the cerebrum's two hemispheres into four separate lobes. The *frontal lobe* lies closest to the forehead, and a crevice called the *central fissure*, which runs from one hemisphere to the other, separates the frontal lobe from the *parietal lobe*. Directly behind the parietal lobe, at the very back of the head, is the *occipital lobe*. The *temporal lobe* is below the frontal and parietal lobes, separated from them by the *sylvian fissure*, which runs along the side of the brain and is located toward the back. Each of the four lobes is distinguished from the others by the specific functions it performs.

Researchers have used a number of methods to learn the tasks carried out by different areas of the cerebrum, one of which involves studying the effects of damage to specific parts of the brain. One of the leading pioneers in this approach was British neurologist John Hughlings Jackson, who studied speech defects caused by brain damage as

Thinking Machines

Growing insight into the human mind is being used to build more effective computers and, slowly, to help scientists develop a machine with *artificial intelligence*, that is, one that thinks the way people do.

Computers are often thought of as "superbrains," but in many respects they are actually quite inefficient when compared to the human thinking machine. Even today's best computers cannot do what the human brain does: solve a problem by finding a connection between seemingly unrelated ideas.

The majority of computers—from personal models to large, industrial mainframes—operate sequentially, performing their work one step at a time according to a fixed set of rules. These machines have a single *central processing unit* carrying out all tasks. The most sophisticated versions of these computers rely on speed to accomplish their work. The brain, however, takes a more sophisticated approach to handling input. Although a neuron is perhaps 100,000 times slower than a typical computer switch, it makes multiple contacts with other neurons. As a result, human thought relies on the number of connections between neurons, not the speed at which the individual cells function.

There is, however, an advanced form of computer that uses a large number of processing units with the ability to tackle the same problem together, a procedure known as *parallel processing*. Moreover, scientists are now trying to take this particular technology a step further by producing computers fitted with an electronic *neural network* designed to simulate brain function.

Neural networks emulate the intricate connections of the brain, substituting electronic components for neurons. The *neuronal units* that make up a neural network are connected to each other in a complex web so that each unit receives signals from many others.

Computer neural networks share certain advantages with the brain. One is that because the units making up the neural network are interconnected, they can share data and perform their duties simultaneously, which means that if one or a few units break down, the overall system still can complete its work. In addition, a neural network can be programmed to learn in much the same way that research suggests the brain learns (see Chapter 6). Successful completion of a task strengthens the connections between the units responsible so that when called upon to do the same job again, the units perform even faster. If the units produce an incorrect answer, the connection between them is weakened. Like a child, a neural network learns from its own mistakes.

A standard strategy for teaching a job to an electronic neural network is to give it a set of rules to follow. If, for example, the task is to cross the street safely, a good set of rules would be: Stop at the edge of the sidewalk, then look both left and right. If no car is coming from either direction, cross the street.

However, researchers are trying to teach computers much more complicated duties than getting from one sidewalk to another, which means that the computers require a more complex set of directions. These rules are compiled through extensive interviews with human experts involved in the particular field being taught. If, for example, a computer was to be taught speech, the programming would include a complete dictionary and a long set of rules concerning grammar and pronunciation.

Carver A. Mead, a neural network researcher at the California Institute of Technology, has been working with colleagues on an ambitious goal: developing a neural network that can be integrated into an electronic vision system. Humans and other living creatures can take in complicated scenes at a glance, at the same time adjusting to different shades of lighting and extracting objects of interest from the background. By comparison, it has been a major challenge to develop a computer system possessing even the most basic vision. Yet a computer able to recognize important patterns in real-life scenes would have a myriad of applications, from processing radar signals to improving burglar alarm systems. Mead's group has built the electronic equivalent of a retina, with tens of thousands of transistors corresponding to the rods and cones of the eye. It is a very primitive device, Mead says, but it is "the first step in simulating the computation that your brain does to process a visual image."

The ultimate goal of neural network research is to create a machine that can match or exceed the capabilities of the human brain. Although the idea may sound ominous to some, in reality it verifies just how effective a machine the human mind truly is.

well as muscle spasms resulting from epilepsy. He was one of the first to realize that epilepsy is caused by the spontaneous firing of groups of neurons.

An epileptic seizure often begins with what is called an aura. This can be a hallucination in which the patient experiences strange visions, smells, or sounds; a feeling of dizziness; tingling in a limb; or some other odd feeling. Jackson methodically listed the nature of the auras experienced by individuals with epilepsy and, after a patient's death, would examine his or her brain; if he found a lesion, he reasoned that the area where the lesion was located controlled the types of sensations experienced in the aura, such as touch, smell, hearing, and vision.

The next step, taken by other researchers, was to stimulate the living brain electrically in order to map its functions. This research was first carried out on dogs; then, in the early 20th century, several scientists, including Harvey Cushing in the United States, began to work with human patients undergoing neurosurgery. Although at first glance such research may appear inhumane, the procedure is in fact painless: The brain has no pain receptors, so a dog or a human whose skull has been opened for surgery feels nothing when electrodes are applied to the cortex.

To perform brain surgery, a physician must locate the exact section of the cerebral hemisphere needing repair; this is best done by electrical stimulation. Montreal neurosurgeon Wilder Penfield helped pioneer this technique in the late 1920s. He, too, began by methodically exploring the cerebral hemispheres, this time with *microelectrodes*. He found that visual hallucinations were caused by stimulation of the back of the occipital lobe and that auditory hallucinations originated deep in the temporal lobe. Penfield's exploration of the temporal lobe also found centers for such emotions as fear, depression, and sorrow—all of which can be felt when brain centers are stimulated electrically. Under electrical stimulation, some of his patients experienced vivid hallucinations, complete in all details of sound, sight, and smell.

In addition, by carefully stimulating small areas in the region of the brain responsible for movement, Penfield found the centers responsible for operating specific parts of the body, including the hands, fingers, lips, and mouth. These areas are organized according to the complexity and sensitivity of the body parts they control; the centers devoted to the hands, lips, and tongue are the largest. Ultimately, Penfield refined his stimulation technique until it could be used routinely to remove the abnormal region from the brain of epileptic patients.

Though the mapping of specific functions to areas of the brain is far from complete, much is now known. The frontal lobe is involved with conscious muscle control, from legs to head. The parietal lobe receives sensory information from skin and muscles, and the occipital lobe contains a large region devoted to vision. Speech control is located within the temporal lobe. Brain centers for taste and smell are on the underside of the hemispheres. Scientists have also been able to locate *primary areas* within the lobes, where most lobe activity is located.

Many scientists believe that not only do the four lobes within each hemisphere perform separate jobs, but each hemisphere carries out certain functions that the other does not. This line of thought was

Harvey Cushing (1869–1939) was a pioneer in neurosurgery. In the early 20th century, he began electrically stimulating the living brain during surgery in order to map its functions.

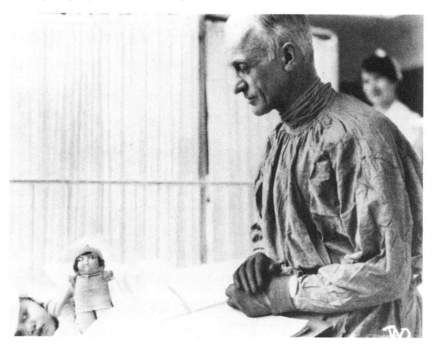

Using microelectrodes to explore the cerebral hemispheres of patients undergoing surgery, Wilder Penfield (1891–1976) found that visual hallucinations can be produced by stimulating the back of the occipital lobe.

pioneered by the 19th-century French pathologist Paul Broca. He was the first scientist to recognize that the left side of the brain in most people is specialized for speech. Broca studied 22 patients who were suffering from brain damage that left them unable to speak, and in every case he found damage to the left hemisphere. Damage to the right hemisphere, by contrast, did not cause language deficiencies. Building on Broca's work, Carl Wernicke, a German neurologist, located a section of the left temporal lobe that is essential for understanding speech.

Although the hemispheres have different capabilities, the various primary areas within the two hemispheres do communicate with each other. Because the outside world provides the brain with so many complex stimuli—mixtures of sight, sound, smell, and movement—the brain has developed in a way that allows all areas to become aware of the stimuli and to coordinate a response. The primary areas are not really concerned with only one sensation. For example, incoming stimuli from touch and pain are mingled in another part of the forebrain, the *thalamus*, which sends signals to many primary areas at once. In addition, a visual stimulus also affects the primary area concerned with hearing.

Each of the primary areas is surrounded by a *secondary*, "parasensory" region. The output of a primary brain center goes only to its secondary area; each neuron of the primary area is connected to many neurons of the secondary area. The secondary areas in one hemisphere are linked to each other and to other regions of the cortex called *association areas*. Finally, secondary areas in the two hemispheres are linked to each other by nerve fibers. The connection between the two sides of the brain is provided mainly by a thick bridge of fibers called the *corpus callosum*, located deep inside the cerebrum.

Beneath each hemisphere reside two groups of brain centers. One group is the *limbic system*, which includes the thalamus, corpus callosum, *amygdala*, and *hippocampus*. The limbic system helps control memory and plays a vital role in human emotions. In a sense, it balances raw emotional feelings with the rational thoughts of the cerebrum. The other group of brain centers consists of the *basal ganglia*, four nerve cell clusters that help to control physical movements by relaying messages from the cortex to an area of the brain called the *brainstem*, a three-inch stretch of nerve fibers connecting the brain to the spinal cord.

Also deep inside the cerebrum, surrounded by the limbic system and sitting above the brainstem, are the *hypothalamus*, *pituitary gland*, and *pineal gland*. These are very small but important brain centers. The hypothalamus, which sits below the two thalami of the limbic system, has a number of functions, including regulating body temperature, breathing rate, hunger, and thirst and influencing blood pressure and the development of secondary sex characteristics.

Under the hypothalamus is a little knoblike stalk, the pituitary gland. For a long time, the pituitary was known as the master gland, the source of hormones that controlled the output of the body's other hormone-secreting glands—those belonging to the *endocrine system*. It is now known that the pituitary is controlled by the hypothalamus, which secretes a number of hormones that modulate the activity of the pituitary. The function of the pineal gland, however, remains a mystery.

The Midbrain

Underneath the forebrain is an inch-long stretch of nerve fibers called the midbrain, which contains centers that receive messages from the inner ear, the eyes, and the cerebrum. The midbrain is also involved in eye movement and controls some reflex activities, such as adjustment

Deep inside the cerebral cortex, surrounded by the various structures of the limbic system, are important brain centers, such as the hypothalamus and the pituitary gland.

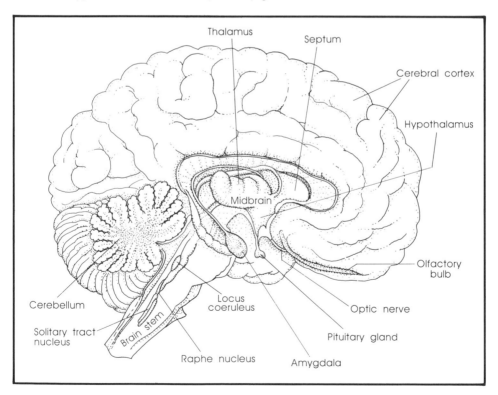

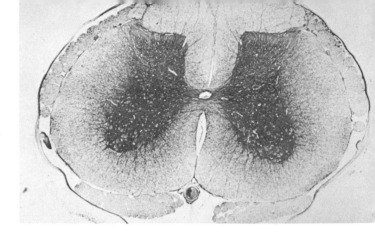

In a cross section of the spinal cord, gray matter appears butterfly-shaped at the center of the spine.

of the size of the eye's pupil. In addition, the midbrain contains a dark area called the *substantia nigra* that helps coordinate movement and muscle tone.

The Hindbrain

The hindbrain comprises the *cerebellum* as well as all parts of the brainstem except the midbrain. These include the *pons*, an inch-wide bridge of cells below the midbrain that serves as a link between the forebrain and the cerebellum; the *reticular formation*; and the *medulla oblongata*. The cerebellum, which is the largest part of the hindbrain and accounts for an eighth of the brain's total mass, is a cabbage-shaped structure divided into two hemispheres. (*Cerebellum* in fact means "little cerebrum," a name derived from its resemblance to the forebrain.)

The cerebellum is involved in controlling bodily position and muscular coordination. It is also believed to play a role in emotions such as pleasure and anger. The cerebellum contains some unusual neurons called Purkinje cells, named for Jan Evangelista Purkinje, the Czech physiologist who first described them in 1837. A single Purkinje cell makes more contacts than any other type of nerve cell—it may be connected to more than 100,000 nerve fibers.

The medulla oblongata is the lowermost part of the brainstem. It has reflex centers that control basic functions including heartbeat, blood pressure, breathing, swallowing, and sneezing. The medulla is also the way station for messages between brain and body. Through the medulla pass all the nerve fibers carrying messages to and from the muscles; some of those fibers terminate in the medulla, whereas others run through to the forebrain.

At the rear of the medulla is the reticular formation, a cluster of neurons that serves as the brain's alarm system. The reticular formation responds to any stimulus, from the smell of morning coffee to the sight of fire, by alerting the forebrain that action is necessary. It also organizes sleep and waking, stopping messages to the brain centers that control consciousness when sleep is necessary and sending them through when wakefulness is needed.

THE SPINAL CORD

Below the cerebellum and connected to the brainstem is the spinal cord, the second component of the central nervous system. The spinal cord is a cylinder of nerve cell tissue about 18 inches long. Like the cerebrum, the spinal cord is composed of both white matter and gray matter. In a cross section of the spinal cord, the gray matter appears butterfly-shaped at the center of the spine, surrounded by white matter. The spinal cord, as well as the brain, is bathed in cerebrospinal fluid and wrapped in three layers of tissue called the *meninges*. The cord is also encased in a series of 33 bones, or vertebrae, which compose the spinal column.

Any messages sent to the brain from the body or vice versa travel by way of the spinal cord. This system of relaying messages is vital to the nervous system for the brain cannot control what its neurons cannot contact. For example, if the spinal cord is severed by a bullet or by an injury sustained in a bad fall, all body functions controlled by the part of the spine below the point of injury will become paralyzed and insensitive. Such an injury may even prove fatal. The spinal cord is as vital as the brain to the functions of the whole body, whether those functions are motor or sensory, conscious or unconscious.

CHAPTER 3

THE SENSES

Neurons both inside and outside the central nervous system enable humans to perceive the world's vital features, such as color, shape, sound, smell, taste, and texture. Those nerves and neurons outside the brain and spinal cord compose the peripheral nervous system, relaying to the brain what the body experiences and carrying back messages telling the body how to respond.

PERIPHERAL NERVOUS SYSTEM

The peripheral nervous system includes 43 pairs of nerves (which, as discussed previously, are bundles of axons), each containing *afferent* fibers, which carry signals to the central nervous system, and *efferent* fibers, which carry signals away from the central nervous system to the body. There are 31 pairs of *spinal nerves* and 12 pairs of *cranial nerves*.

Spinal Nerves

On both sides of the spinal cord, a nerve emerges through a gap between two vertebrae. Just outside the cord, each of these spinal nerves forks into two bundles. One consists of only sensory, or afferent, fibers involved in detecting aspects of touch such as pain and temperature.

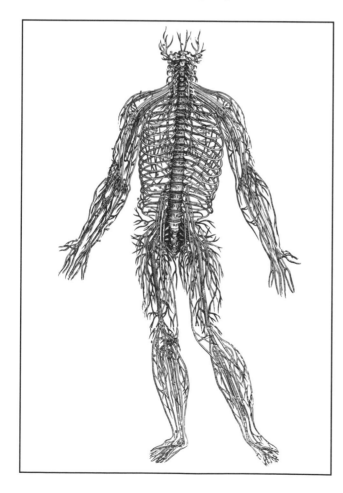

The Belgian anatomist Andreas Vesalius (1514–64) prepared drawings of the human body based on his own dissections of human cadavers. Here he has illustrated the body's network of peripheral nerves.

The other fork is made up of motor, or efferent, fibers. Sensory fibers carry signals from sensory receptors in the skin, muscles, and other parts of the body to the spinal cord; motor fibers carry signals out from the spinal cord to muscles and glands. The sensory branch of one nerve enters the cord between the vertebrae toward the back of the spine, at what is called the *dorsal root* of the spinal cord. The motor nerve exits from the *ventral root*, toward the front side of the spinal column.

Cranial Nerves

The cranial nerves originate in the head and branch off from the brainstem. Numbered from 1 to 12, they are the *olfactory, optic, vestibulocochlear, trochlear, abducens, accessory, hypoglossal, trigeminal, oculomotor, facial, glossopharyngeal,* and *vagus* nerves. All of these nerves have at least one of four functions: They are involved in providing vision, hearing, smell, taste, touch, and/or balance (the optic, vestibulocochlear, and olfactory nerves are included in this group); control certain skeletal muscles; inform the brain about the position of the body; or regulate glands, smooth muscle, or cardiac muscle.

VISION

Beginning with the primitive, light-sensitive cells of simple animals, vision has developed into a complex system of cooperation between the eye and the brain. The human eye is, of course, one of the best examples of this evolution (although not necessarily *the* best, because animals such as hawks and eagles have even sharper vision, a gift that enables them to seek prey while in flight).

The human eye allows light to enter through an adjustable opening called the *pupil*. It then uses a flexible lens to focus that light on the retina, at the back of the eye. The retina has three layers of cells: dark pigment cells, which absorb excess light; light-sensitive receptor cells; and signal-processing cells.

About 90% of the receptor cells are very sensitive to faint light but provide the brain with only shades of gray vision. Because of their shape, these cells are called *rods*. The other receptor cells, called *cones*, are of three types, each sensitive to one color. As long ago as 1807, British physician Thomas Young proposed that the eye has three kinds of receptors, each sensitive to either red, green, or violet color. More than 150 years later, scientists proved that he was virtually correct by finding 3 kinds of cone cells in the retina, each sensitive to either red, green, or blue wavelengths. (The other colors that humans see are subtle blends of these three.) However, the world is colorful only when lit. When, for example, the light of the sun activates the cells, a person with normal vision can see many colors. In the evening, though, the light is too faint to activate cone cells, so the world appears to lose its color. At this point, the rods become more active than the cones, and the world appears as shades of gray.

Light reaching the retinal cells sets off electrochemical signals that, in turn, stimulate the retina's *ganglionic layer*, which is made up of neurons that have converged to form the two optic nerves. From the right half of each eye, fibers from the optic nerves travel to the right thalamus, then to the *visual cortex*, that part of the cortex concerned with vision. Neurons on the left side of each eye travel to the left

A scanning electron micrograph of rods and cones, magnified 2,500 times. Cones detect color when activated by bright light; rods provide the brain with shades of gray, a function most important at night.

thalamus and left visual cortex. Thus, the centers in the two occipital lobes each get signals from both eyes—an important factor in binocular vision, providing humans with better perception of depth and a complete field of view.

The primary visual area on each side of the brain mirrors the retina completely, in a one-to-one correspondence between the cells of the retina and neurons in the cortex. There is another point-to-point mirror in both secondary visual areas and yet another area in the front part of each temporal lobe, where some neurons receive signals from the entire visual field. Neurons in the vision centers of the cortex respond to different stimuli. The cortex has a layer of cells that are sensitive to orientation; for example, one will respond to a line at an angle of 45 degrees to the horizon, another to a line at a 90 degree angle. Other neurons respond to a line that moves in specific directions. Thus, the eye not only perceives color and shape but is also able to detect movement.

How the cerebral cortex processes all of these signals to produce the sense of vision is still uncertain. However, scientists have gotten clues from what is called an "ambiguous" figure, an image that can be seen as two different things but is perceived by the human eye as one thing or the other. The eye never sees both possible versions at the same time. In the case of one well-known ambiguous figure, for example, one person may see the image of a white vase against a black background; another person may see the silhouette of two human profiles facing each other, separated by a white background. Some scientists use this evidence to support what is called the *Gestalt theory*, which says that the brain tends to group incoming signals into complete images, to see the world in complete patterns that are built into the brain. Just how these patterns are created may be answered at least partially by a Nobel Prize–winning theory developed by researchers David Hubel and Torsten Wiesel: It suggests that the brain comprehends an object as a series of lines, edges, and light and dark bars, which the brain then assembles into a complete image.

HEARING

The stimulus for hearing is mechanical motion. Sound consists of airwaves that cause vibrations of the *eardrum*, a thin membrane inside the ear. These vibrations are transmitted by the *ossicles*, three small bones in the middle ear, to the *cochlea*, a snail-shaped organ in the inner ear. Inside the cochlea is a tube filled with fluid, and on the outer membrane of the tube are more than 20,000 delicate *hair cells*. Vibrations pass through the fluid within the tube, disturbing the hair cells which, in turn, stimulate nerve cells to fire. Signals are carried first to two sections of the midbrain, the *inferior colliculus* and the *medial geniculate nucleus*, and then to cortical neurons in the temporal lobes. Nerve cell impulses from the right ear go mainly to the left side of the brain and vice versa.

Unlike the neurons in the visual area of the cortex, those for hearing do not have a one-to-one correspondence with the receptor cells of the cochlea. Like the visual area, however, the auditory area has specialized neurons; some, for example, respond to the start or end of a sound, some to a sound of a particular duration, some to changes in frequency. Many neurons are sensitive to the differences in the direction of a sound, enabling a person to determine the source of the sound.

SMELL AND TASTE

The sense of smell, unlike vision and hearing, is a response to chemical stimuli. The receptors for odors are concentrated in an area of mucous membrane at the top of the nose. These *olfactory sensors* are believed to respond primarily to molecular shapes, although the way atoms move within a molecule and the way the molecules combine with receptor molecules also appear to play a role in the detection of odors. Each receptor cell sends out a thin projection into the mucus, and each projection has many *cilia*, tiny hairs that detect molecules. The nerve cells that carry signals from the receptors terminate on the *olfactory bulbs*, two knoblike structures that project from the olfactory area of the cortex.

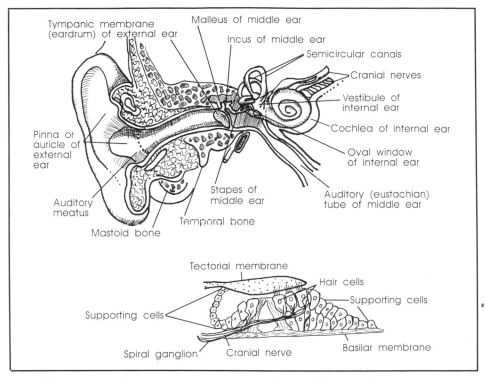

Tympanic membrane (eardrum) of external ear
Malleus of middle ear
Incus of middle ear
Semicircular canals
Cranial nerves
Vestibule of internal ear
Cochlea of internal ear
Oval window of internal ear
Pinna or auricle of external ear
Auditory (eustachian) tube of middle ear
Auditory meatus
Stapes of middle ear
Temporal bone
Mastoid bone

Tectorial membrane
Hair cells
Supporting cells
Supporting cells
Spiral ganglion
Cranial nerve
Basilar membrane

Sound is created when sound waves cause the eardrum to vibrate. When these vibrations reach the cochlea, hair cells stimulate neurons to fire, sending messages via cranial nerves to the brain.

There are two routes to the olfactory sensors: through the nose or up the back of the throat. Odors from inhalation come in through the nose, whereas odors from food and drink follow the other route. To reach the receptors, a molecule must be carried to them by air; it then dissolves in the mucus that coats the inside of the nasal cavity. If a cold or other infection thickens the mucus, preventing the dissolved molecules from penetrating to the receptors, the sense of smell is diminished, and because the smell of food contributes to the enjoyment of its taste, the sense of taste will seem diminished as well. The receptors for odors are located in the layer of epithelium that lines the nasal cavity.

The olfactory bulbs occupy only a small part of the human brain but are much more prominent in animals such as dogs, for whom smell is the main source of sensory information. Although a human's sense of smell is not as well developed as that of many other animals, it has some impressive characteristics. Humans can detect some 5,000 different odors, in amazingly small concentrations. For example, *mercaptans*, sulfur-containing molecules, can be detected in a concentration measured in parts per million. One such mercaptan is added to natural gas so that people may be warned of leaks.

Like the sense of smell, taste perception is also chemically stimulated, and scientists have a good idea of how taste is detected. Receptors for taste are grouped into structures called *taste buds* that are found on the surface of the tongue. Food particles must first be dissolved by saliva before any molecules can bind to receptors. When this binding occurs, an afferent neuron is stimulated, and the sensation of taste is conveyed by the facial or glossopharyngeal cranial nerves to the medulla, thalamus, and cortex. However, scientists are still unsure of how these signals are processed after reaching their destinations.

TOUCH

The skin is studded with receptors that detect the nature, intensity, and location of any touch. Exactly how many different types of receptors are in the skin is unclear. Some receptors are nerve endings responsible for detecting pain and temperature. Other receptors are nerve endings that respond to any mechanical force applied to the skin. These *mechanoreceptors* are generally larger than the temperature- and pain-detecting receptors. They act in much the same way as the mouthpiece of a telephone, transforming a mechanical movement into an electrical impulse.

Impulses from mechanoreceptors travel to the back part of the spinal cord, called the *dorsal horn*. They continue upward through the brainstem, then cross to the opposite side of the body to one of the thalami. Signals are then sent to the cortex, where they are received by neurons mapping the specific parts of the body.

The nervous system uses a mechanism called *surround inhibition* to help pinpoint the area of skin being stimulated. As neurons from that point send signals to the spinal cord, impulses originating from neighboring areas are inhibited, which means that messages from the stimulated area stand out better against this "silent" background.

Pain

Pain, like other senses, has a system of sensors that gathers data and sends signals via specialized nerves to brain centers, there triggering a response. Pain can actually be regarded, however, as a specialized form of the sense of touch. Whereas other sensory receptors respond to continuous stimulation by reducing the rate of firing, pain receptors adapt slightly or not at all to continuous stimulation because the signals they send are so urgent and important.

Different sensations can cause pain. There are nerve fibers called *nociceptors* that are specific for painful stimuli, but overstimulation of receptors for pressure or temperature can also result in pain. The nerve fibers from these receptors run to the dorsal horn of the spinal cord, where they make synaptic contact with a variety of neurons. Because some of the spinal cord neurons receive signals from receptors in the skin, the muscles, and internal organs, the central nervous system is not always exactly sure where the pain messages are coming from. The body may seem to "ache all over."

One widely accepted theory proposed by Ronald Melzack of McGill University in Montreal and Patrick Wall of the Massachusetts Institute of Technology states that some nerve cells in the dorsal horn act as a "gate" for pain signals. Some messages to these cells open the gate, sending pain signals through; others close it, blocking the transmission of pain signals—in other words, the stimulation of certain receptors sends messages to close the gate so that pain is not perceived. This is one way to explain the pain-relieving attributes of *acupuncture*, in which needles are stuck into carefully selected points on the body. The needles appear to stimulate the kind of pain sensors that close the gate.

The brain itself causes a different sort of pain inhibition by producing natural opiates, which are substances that help relieve discomfort. *Enkephalins* and *endorphins* were discovered in the 1970s by scientists who questioned why opiates such as morphine and heroin, which are derived from plants, have such a profound effect on humans—not only relieving pain but also, if taken often enough, causing addiction. Several neuroscientists, among them Solomon Snyder and Candace

Pert of Johns Hopkins University, discovered that nerve cells in the brain and spinal cord have opiate receptors in their cell membranes—molecules that respond to enkephalins and endorphins. Natural opiates bind to the receptors and reduce the rate at which the neurons fire, thus decreasing the brain's perception of pain.

Not long after the discovery of opiate receptors, John Hughes and Hans Kosterlitz of the University of Aberdeen in Scotland isolated the first enkephalins, two molecules whose shape is mimicked by plant opiates. The other natural opiates, the endorphins, were isolated by Snyder and researchers at several other laboratories. These discoveries

Dr. Henry Beecher's study of soldiers wounded in the Battle of Anzio during World War II helped show that different circumstances apparently affect how a person perceives pain.

led to an explanation of opiate addiction. When someone takes an artificial opiate, the body reduces its production of enkephalins and endorphins, so that the user comes to rely on the outside source. If that artificial supply stops, the result is an agonizing set of withdrawal symptoms that persist until the body begins making its own opiates again.

Natural opiates appear to be activated by a number of stimuli, including stress, sometimes causing euphoric feelings—as in the case of the "runner's high" produced when natural opiates are activated by strenuous exercise. Because they seem to turn off the brain's recognition of pain signals, opiates may also be responsible for the well-known phenomenon in which many individuals, at moments of severe shock, do not feel pain.

Pain is a complex feeling, because it depends in part on individual expectations and reactions: A situation that one person finds intensely painful may hardly bother someone else, or a stimulus may cause pain in one situation but not in another. For example, in a study of 150 American soldiers wounded in the battle of Anzio during World War II, Dr. Henry Beecher of Harvard University found that only one-third asked for drugs such as morphine, an extract of opium. When Beecher studied 150 men who underwent surgery in peacetime, he found that 80% requested pain-relieving drugs. The different circumstances apparently affected their perception of pain.

Temperature

Perceiving temperature can also be considered a specialized form of the sense of touch. There are two kinds of receptors in the skin that are tailored to sense temperature: cold receptors near the surface of the skin, in the *epidermis*, and heat receptors deeper in the skin, in the layer called the *dermis*. Heat receptors fire when the skin is warmed and stop when it is cooled; conversely, cold receptors fire when the skin is cooled and stop when it is warmed.

Temperature receptors are needed to keep the body's internal temperature within the fairly narrow limits for which nature has designed it, roughly 86 to 113 degrees Fahrenheit (30 to 45 degrees Celsius). As sensory nerves detect a drop in temperature, the nervous system sends out signals that slow blood circulation to the outer parts of the body and send more blood to the inner organs to keep them warm. When the temperature goes up, the nervous system responds by causing blood vessels in the skin to dilate so that heat can escape from the body and by causing the skin to perspire—sweat cools the body as it evaporates. At intermediate temperatures, both kinds of sensors send out fewer signals.

CHAPTER 4

MOTOR CONTROL

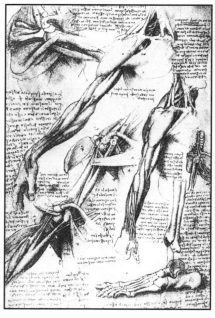

Drawing by Leonardo da Vinci
(1452–1519)

Almost all voluntary movements are made in response to stimuli from the environment—sights, sounds, smells, and more. The brain processes messages received from the sensory organs and then determines the proper response. If movement is necessary, the brain sends messages to the spinal cord, which relays them via the motor neurons to skeletal muscles, the muscles that make bones move.

Muscles are generally arranged in pairs. As a rule, when one member of a pair contracts, the other relaxes. Skeletal muscles that bend bones toward each other are called *flexors*. Muscles that extend bones outward are called *extensors*. For every extensor action there is an equal and opposite flexor reaction. For example, when pointing a finger, flexors contract and extensors relax. When straightening the finger, the flexors relax and the extensors contract. None of this could happen without the help of neurons.

SPINAL CORD REFLEXES

Although conscious movement, such as pointing a finger, requires that the brain command the skeletal muscles to contract and relax, the spinal cord is capable of handling some simple muscular responses on its own. Touching a hot stove with a finger, for example, stimulates pain receptors. An impulse travels along sensory fibers to neurons in the spinal cord. Next, signals travel from these nerve cells to the motor neurons that flex muscles, causing the arm to move away from the stove. This protective mechanism is called a *flexion reflex*.

Another kind of reflex action can be demonstrated when the knee is tapped just below the kneecap. This time the message runs to the spinal cord and then straight back to the knee, activating the muscles that jerk the leg forward. The entire response, known as the *stretch reflex*, occurs in a fraction of a second. This type of circuit is designed to maintain posture and muscle tone during movement.

Much of the control of skeletal muscles is carried out by reflex circuits that never get beyond the spinal cord. The simple act of standing, for example, depends on a reflex circuit that makes all the muscles of the legs contract at once. Other activities, such as walking, may seem as simple but are actually much more complicated.

WHEN NERVE MEETS MUSCLE

Movement depends on both the sensory and motor activity of the peripheral nervous system. A constant stream of signals goes from *proprioceptors*, sensory receptors in the muscles and joints, to the spinal cord. Proprioceptors in the joints have specialized receptors that fire only under some type of strain, as when the joint is put into an extremely unusual position. Those in the muscles detect movement.

Along with regular muscle bundles, which contract and relax to cause movement, are other muscle bundles called *spindle organs*. The spindle organs are connected to and move with regular muscle bundles in order to help the brain keep track of the body's motion. This is accomplished with the help of two kinds of afferent sensory nerve fibers, or axons, called *primary* and *secondary fibers*, attached to the spindles. Primary nerve fibers are literally wrapped around the center of spindle muscle fibers; secondary fibers are attached to the ends of these muscle fibers. Every time a regular muscle bundle contracts or relaxes, the spindle organ moves with it, causing the attached axons to stretch or relax. The nerve fibers, in turn, send signals to the spinal cord. Primary nerve fibers are the fastest conducting axons in the body; their receptors fire when muscle movement starts or stops. Secondary fiber receptors fire as long as the muscle continues to stretch. Other sensory fibers end in a set of receptors called the *Golgi tendon organs* (named for the Italian researcher) which, as their name implies, are located in the tendons attached to muscles. They send signals only when a muscle contracts.

When messages from these various receptors reach the spinal cord, an appropriate response is signaled back to the muscles by way of motor neurons. Those signals arrive at *neuromuscular* junctions, where motor neurons meet the muscles. The neuromuscular junction synapse, however, is a bit different from others because at the end of each motor neuron is a *motor end plate*, which makes contact with the membrane that covers a muscle fiber. Every such neuromuscular synapse uses the same neurotransmitter, acetylcholine. When a motor neuron releases acetylcholine, the membrane of the muscle fiber depolarizes, causing the muscle fiber to contract. That contraction is the essence of muscle activity.

ORGANS OF BALANCE

To remain standing or to move involves not only the spinal cord, peripheral nerves, and muscles but also the eyes and ears. For example,

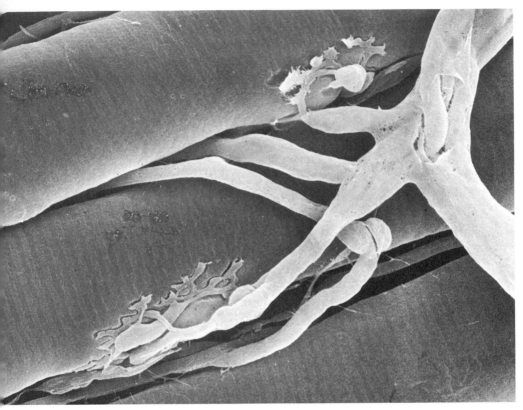

This scanning electron micrograph reveals that the neuromuscular junction is like no other synapse. The motor neuron actually contacts its target, the muscle fiber, via the motor end plate.

in addition to containing organs responsible for hearing, the inner ear also holds the *labyrinth*, a complex set of organs that maintain balance.

The labyrinth has three fluid-filled loops of bone, the *semicircular canals*, oriented at right angles to each other. Tiny hairs, or cilia, enable the semicircular canals to sense rotational motion such as turning around or turning one's head to one side. With the help of two other organs, the *utricle* and the *saccule*, the labyrinth also keeps balance during "linear motion," that is, movement directly from one point to another, such as when one walks in a straight line or jumps off a stool. The semicircular canals stick out from the utricle and saccule, which, along with fluid, also contain grains of material called *otoliths*. When someone moves in a straight line forward or down, the otoliths move upward and the hairs straighten, informing the brain of the head's position during this movement.

The labyrinth also tells the eyes of the movements made by the head. This enables the eye to adjust and maintain a stable image while the body is moving. If adjustments were not made by the eyes, the images produced on the retina would change so rapidly that vision would be impaired, even during the slightest movement of the head.

In addition, visual signals combine with signals from the proprioceptors to keep the central nervous system informed about position so that skeletal muscles can make their own adjustments. Sometimes, however, the visual system detects motion but gets no confirmation from other sensory organs, and this can cause confusion. For example, people in a stationary train that is next to a moving train may not be able to distinguish whether their train is moving backward or the other train is moving forward.

THE CEREBELLUM AND BASAL GANGLIA

The cerebellum appears to coordinate the reflexes that maintain balance. Another of its functions is to control *muscle tone*, keeping muscle contraction and relaxation within proper bounds. To do this, the cerebellum helps coordinate input from a number of sensory centers in the cerebral hemispheres. Vision, for example, plays a role in muscle tone. A person may perceive an object to be much heavier or lighter than it actually is—a block of aluminum may look like lead, for instance. As the object is placed in the person's hand, the hand will move upward involuntarily, overcompensating for the weight of the object because the visual system has prepared the arm to handle an object much heavier than it turned out to be.

Conscious motor activity, such as turning a page or taking a step, originates in the cortex. It is believed that when these signals travel to the appropriate motor neurons, duplicate instructions are sent to the cerebellum, which also gets signals from the sensing organs in the muscles. The cerebellum compares the input and output signals and issues modifying commands that keep the system working smoothly.

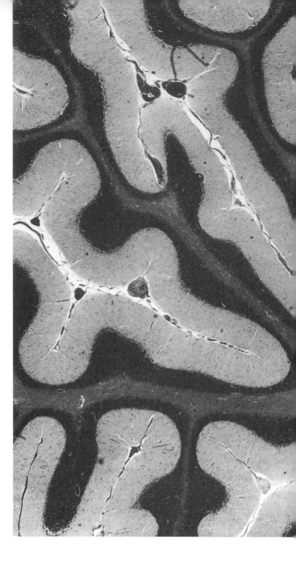

This transverse section shows that, like the cerebrum, the cerebellum has many deep convolutions. The cerebellum, however, is concerned with the coordination of muscles and the maintenance of equilibrium.

The basal ganglia also appear to play some role in coordinating movement. However, it is not entirely clear how either the basal ganglia or the cerebellum performs this function. Diseases of the basal ganglia, including *Parkinson's disease* and *Huntington's chorea*, are characterized by a severe loss of motor control, just as there is a substantial loss of control when the cerebellum does not function properly. An individual can still walk and carry out basic functions but does so clumsily and inefficiently. Walking becomes staggered; reaching for an object becomes an ill-controlled grope.

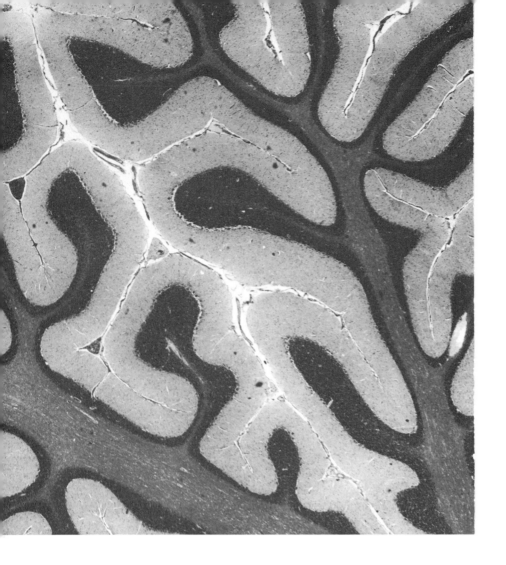

THE CORTEX

The cerebrum is also involved in motor control but is strongly influenced by the cerebellum, which controls the direction, force, and rate of movement. Through one pathway to the spinal cord and brainstem, the motor cortex controls the more complex learned behaviors such as playing the violin or swinging a golf club with precision. Through another pathway, the cortex smooths the movement of limbs and maintains the act of walking. Although walking is controlled by a lower part of the brain, it is the cortex that decides whether the body will start or stop walking. It sends these messages through the reticular formation to the muscles that adjust posture.

Even innate, or built-in, movements such as walking require the learning and memory functions of the cortex to provide precise, sophisticated use of the muscles. For example, a baby makes fumbling movements at first but improves performance with practice. If something interferes with this learning process, the nervous system never acquires the circuitry needed to carry out activities with complete dexterity.

CHAPTER 5

THE AUTONOMIC NERVOUS SYSTEM

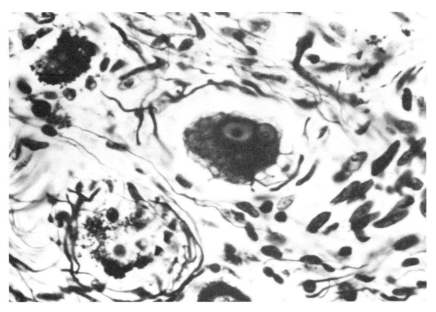

A microphotograph of a neuron from a sympathetic ganglion, magnified 400 times

Much of what the body does is controlled by the biological equivalent of an automatic pilot. A young girl relaxing in a comfortable chair, absorbed by the narrative of a good book, may appear to be physically inactive, but her body is hard at work. While she sits reading, she also digests a previous meal. If the room is very hot, she perspires. If someone else in the room makes a loud noise, she may jump to her feet, alarmed and alert. All these unconscious, instinctive activities are controlled by the autonomic nervous system.

NEURONS

All autonomic neurons are part of the peripheral nervous system. Instead of directly causing skeletal muscles to move, however, they carry messages to *glands*; *cardiac muscle*, which is found in the heart; and *smooth muscle*, which is found in areas such as the stomach, bladder, eyes, and lungs. Focusing of the lens of the eye and the dilation and contraction of the pupil are under autonomic control, for example, as is the dilation and constriction of blood vessels and air passages in the lungs.

However, the autonomic system normally requires help from the central nervous system to do its job. Signals are initially sent through a nerve cell that branches out from the spinal cord and runs to a ganglion, which, as mentioned, is a cluster of nerve cell bodies. Then a second neuron, part of the autonomic system, extends from the ganglion to one of the glands or organs—such as the heart, stomach, or salivary glands—controlled by the system. Because many autonomic nerve cells can extend out from one ganglion, signals traveling to the ganglia from a single spinal cord neuron can spread out through a number of autonomic fibers, like water flowing through a pipe that suddenly branches off in different directions. As a result, signals from one spinal nerve cell can affect many parts of the autonomic system, thereby helping the body keep its various organs working in cooperation with each other.

COMPLEMENTARY PARTS

The Greek physician Galen (129–ca. 199), who, among many other things, tended to the injured gladiators in Pergamum, defined the autonomic nervous system as that which keeps the body in harmony with the environment. Thus, it was initially named the "sympathetic" system, because it was believed to respond to and offer humans protection from their sometimes harsh environment. Eventually, scientists realized that this system actually consisted of two parts; one portion retained the name *sympathetic* and the other became known as the *parasympathetic* nervous system. The sympathetic system governs the body's response to pain, anger, and fear, and the parasympathetic system controls involuntary actions inside the body, such as the secretion of substances and the dilation of blood vessels.

These two parts of the autonomic system usually work together. For example, the intestinal tract is controlled by both sympathetic and parasympathetic signals. After a meal, it is the parasympathetic system that goes into action. It signals digestive juices to flow and the walls of the intestine to begin the rhythmic rippling that moves food along. Then, as food is digested, the sympathetic nervous system goes to work, sending signals that reduce the activity of the digestive tract. Both autonomic divisions are also involved in the functions of the body related to sexual intercourse.

MODIFYING THE INTERNAL ENVIRONMENT

A key element in the autonomic nervous system is the hypothalamus, which helps the autonomic system regulate many aspects of the body's

The Greek physician Galen (129–ca. 199) distinguished the autonomic nervous system as that which keeps the body in harmony with the environment. He named it the "sympathetic" system.

internal environment, such as temperature, water balance, food intake, and the sleep-wake cycle. For example, upon receiving messages from the hypothalamus that the body is uncomfortably warm, the sympathetic nervous system causes blood vessels to dilate, or become larger, so that a certain degree of heat may escape the body. If the temperature rises higher, the vessels become even more dilated, and specialized glands are stimulated to cool the body by secreting sweat. In cold temperatures, blood vessels contract, or become smaller, to reduce heat loss, and as muscles in the skin contract to decrease the amount of skin exposed to the cold, "goose bumps" appear.

Autonomic function is also greatly influenced by one's emotions, which, in turn, are linked to the limbic system. In addition, the autonomic system carries out some of its duties indirectly through the *adrenal medulla*, a gland that helps humans cope with stress. Located at the top of the kidney, it contains two chemicals vital to many autonomic activities: *adrenaline* (which stimulates the heart and increases muscle strength) and *noradrenaline* (which constricts blood vessels and helps transmit nerve signals). The sympathetic nervous system is responsible for stimulating this gland, which in turn releases the two chemicals into the bloodstream, which transports them to all tissues of the body. The chemicals produce the same results as the direct action of sympathetic neurons, but their effects may last 10 times as long.

Response to Stress

In times of stress, the sympathetic nervous system plays the biggest role in autonomic function. For example, the young girl who sits alone in her room, reading a book in the quiet of the evening, may jump to her feet upon hearing a loud noise. Her pupils dilate, her heart beats faster, her breathing quickens, and her blood pressure increases, while blood flow to her intestines and stomach is reduced. Her liver releases a surge of sugar for quick energy, her adrenal glands pump out the hormone adrenaline, and her mouth becomes dry as salivary glands become less active. Overall, her body has responded as it should, for she is ready to either flee or defend herself from danger. Thus, it is the sympathetic nervous system that causes what is known as the *fight-or-flight* reaction associated with anxiety.

The parasympathetic nervous system dominates autonomic function in more relaxed times, keeping the heart beating at a slower pace and keeping blood flowing to the intestines to encourage digestion.

A CONDITIONED RESPONSE

Although the autonomic nervous system usually acts automatically, it is possible to bring some of its functions under control. One method of doing so was demonstrated at the turn of the century by Russian physiologist Ivan Pavlov, who induced what is called a *conditioned response* in dogs. In his most famous series of experiments, Pavlov rang a bell each time he gave food to the dogs. The dogs responded to being fed by salivating. After a while, Pavlov stopped feeding the dogs but kept ringing the bell; the dogs continued to salivate. In these experiments, an autonomic response was "trained" to occur in reaction to a stimulus: The dogs salivated because they had learned to associate the sound of the bell with feeding time.

CONSCIOUS TRAINING OF THE SYSTEM

One exciting development of recent decades is the conscious control of some autonomic functions. This sort of training, called *biofeedback*, has become well established, although it has not lived up to many of the high hopes once held for it. Biofeedback first came to public attention in the late 1960s. The word itself was coined in 1969 to refer to any technique that uses some kind of electronic aid, such as a visual or audio display, to teach a person to control body functions he or she would ordinarily not be aware of, such as heartbeat or brain wave activity. The most prominent series of biofeedback experiments were performed at Rockefeller University by Neal E. Miller and Leo V. DiCara.

Working with rats, Miller and DiCara used sensors to monitor such autonomic functions as blood pressure, heart rate, and intestinal contractions. Rats that changed these functions—for example, by raising

An assistant to the Russian physiologist Ivan Pavlov fills sterilized bottles with gastric juices. By studying conditioned responses in dogs, Pavlov (1849–1936) showed that training can be used to stimulate autonomic activity.

blood pressure or reducing heart rate—were given rewards, a standard way of encouraging certain behavior in animals. In early experiments, the rewards were such things as extra food. Later, the reward was stimulation of a "pleasure center" in the hypothalamus. Eventually, the rats were trained to increase or decrease their heart rate by 20% in as little as 20 minutes.

Even while Miller and DiCara were reporting success with their rodent studies, attempts at human biofeedback training were under way. At Harvard University, Herbert Benson and his colleagues trained six of seven patients to lower their abnormally high blood pressure. At the University of California at San Francisco, Bernard T. Engle trained volunteers to speed up or slow down their heart rate. At the Menninger

Foundation, Elmer Green and colleagues used biofeedback training to help give some relief to headache patients. The pain of migraine headaches is caused by overstretched blood vessels in the brain. By diverting blood to the hands, the Menninger technique lessened pressure in the brain.

Brain Waves

Another area of biofeedback research that caused great excitement in the 1960s and 1970s involved brain waves. In the 1920s, an American researcher, Hans Berger, discovered that it was possible to detect the electrical activity of the brain by attaching electrodes to the scalp. (The resulting record, called an *electroencephalogram* (EEG), is now used by physicians to help diagnose many conditions, including epilepsy and brain tumors.)

After a while, researchers realized that they could distinguish specific brain waves produced during different states of activity. For example, a person produces *alpha waves*, with a frequency of 8 to 13 waves per second, when he or she is relaxing. On the other hand, *beta waves*, which have a higher frequency than alpha waves do, are produced when a person concentrates on an outside stimulus, such as homework. *Delta waves* occur during deep sleep, in infancy, and in people with serious brain disease, whereas *theta waves*, which tend to be the most frequently occurring waves in children aged two to five, are also seen in adults during periods of frustration and in the drowsy period before sleep.

Meditation

Most biofeedback work focused on encouraging the production of alpha waves, and there was a period when great hopes were held for mind training using these waves. A number of researchers related alpha waves to the *meditation* practiced by yoga or Zen Buddhism masters. Studies in Japan showed that Zen monks who had practiced deep meditation for many years could reduce their consumption of oxygen by at least 20%, presumably by exercising some control over the autonomic nervous system. EEG studies showed that the frequency of alpha waves became slower, but the waves became more intense, with higher peaks. Theta waves became prominent in the monks and in yogis during deep meditation.

A technique used by these monks and yogis, *transcendental meditation*, was brought to the United States in the 1960s and was adopted by thousands of Americans. It consists of 2 daily 20-minute sessions during which the individual sits quietly with eyes closed and concentrates on a *mantra*, or short phrase, while clearing the mind of other thoughts.

A number of American researchers, most notably Herbert Benson of Harvard Medical School, have conducted intensive investigations of meditation. Their first goal was to determine whether the same effects seen in the yogis and Zen monks, including reduced oxygen

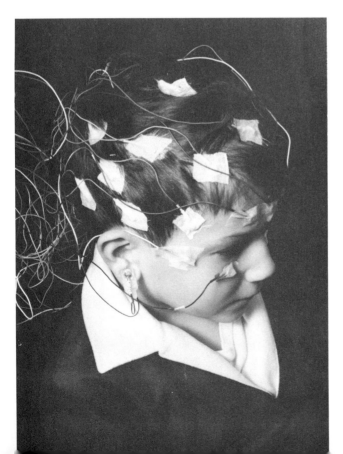

By attaching electrodes to the scalp and recording electrical activity in the brain, physicians can diagnose many conditions, including epilepsy and brain tumors. The resulting record is called an electroencephalogram (EEG).

Meditation, practiced by yoga or Zen Buddhism masters, enables an individual to exercise some control over autonomic functions. Studies in Japan showed that Zen monks could actually reduce their need for oxygen.

consumption, occurred in other people who practiced transcendental meditation. The next step was to find out if alpha wave activity could be controlled through biofeedback training.

Controlling Disease

The major hope for biofeedback training was that it could be used against some diseases, including intestinal disorders and headaches. The thought was that such conditions are caused early in life when the autonomic nervous system is unwittingly trained to respond incorrectly to stress. If people could learn to modify these responses, DiCara wrote in 1970, "it may be possible in effect to 'train' people with certain disorders to get well. Such therapeutic learning should be worth trying on any symptom that is under neural control, that can be continuously monitored and for which a certain direction of change is clearly advisable from a medical point of view."

Even as such hopeful words were written, some limitations to biofeedback began to emerge. For reasons that are still unclear, efforts to repeat the Miller-DiCara experiments with rats became less and less successful. In humans, meanwhile, the clinical effects of biofeedback did not live up to the original expectations. In treatment of high blood pressure, for example, the effects of biofeedback were found to be somewhat lackluster and to fade unless reinforced by constant training sessions. Efforts to train cardiac patients to change their heart rate were also not very successful. Similarly, after an initial burst of widespread enthusiasm, alpha wave training fell into disuse because its benefits were unclear.

Today, there are some established clinical uses of biofeedback. The Menninger Foundation, for example, still uses it to help migraine patients, but such programs remain the exception. Medically, drugs and other conventional treatments have proved to be more effective than biofeedback in changing the function of the autonomic system. In terms of basic research, however, the finding that the body's automatic pilot can be affected by the conscious mind is a lasting contribution to understanding this part of the nervous system.

CHAPTER 6

LEARNING
AND MEMORY

Of all the mind's capabilities, learning and memory may be the most remarkable. A person can recall thousands of facts in a matter of moments—from a Social Security number to a memorable event to the face of a relative. Memories can be revived after being locked up for decades, and the store of them seems inexhaustible. Researchers have been studying the brain for centuries, but only within the past decade or so have they begun to understand the biological mechanisms of learning and memory.

THE ROLE OF
NEUROTRANSMITTERS

The best information on the nature of the physical changes that create memories comes from animal experiments. In these, scientists have looked more or less directly at neurons before and after learning takes place. The best-known series of experiments has been done during the last 30 years by Eric Kandel at Columbia University. Kandel works with the California sea-dwelling snail *Aplysia californica*, whose entire nervous system contains only 20,000 neurons. However, these neurons are large, which allows Kandel to measure what happens within them during the learning process.

Aplysia has indeed been found to have the ability to learn. If touched gently on its siphon, a breathing organ on top of its gill, *Aplysia* retracts the gill slowly. If it is alerted to the possibility of danger (if it is given, say, electric shocks to its tail), the snail quickly covers the siphon and gill with a protective flap of skin.

Sensory and motor nerve cells link the tail and the siphon. When the tail is shocked a number of times, the sensory neurons, the nerve cells at the siphon end of that link, accumulate an unusually large amount of neurotransmitter molecules. Another shock releases these molecules, giving a sudden, strong message to the motor neurons that act on the muscle that pulls the siphon and gill under the protective flap. This is a good model of *sensitization*, a kind of learning that puts the nervous system on alert. For example, because experience has taught some circuits in the human nervous system that the sound of an automobile horn means danger, a person crossing the street may be startled upon hearing such a sound.

There is another kind of learning called *habituation*, which occurs on repeated exposure to a not-very-meaningful stimulus. If, for example, an automobile horn were to go off every five minutes in the street outside a person's room, that person would soon stop paying attention to the sound. In *Aplysia*, Kandel produces habituation by repeated gentle squirts of water on the siphon. After a while, the snail does not respond to the stimulus, because the neurons in that circuit do

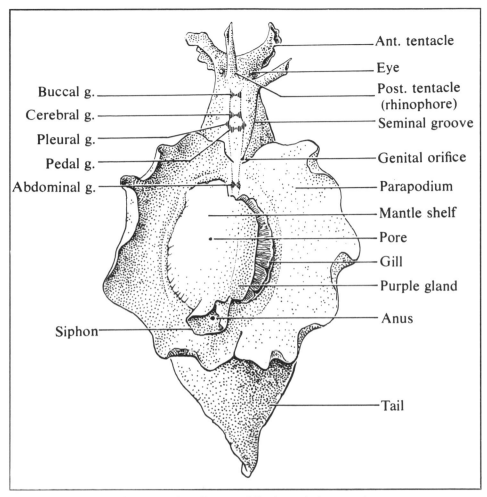

Buccal g.

Cerebral g.

Pleural g.

Pedal g.

Abdominal g.

Siphon

Ant. tentacle

Eye

Post. tentacle
(rhinophore)

Seminal groove

Genital orifice

Parapodium

Mantle shelf

Pore

Gill

Purple gland

Anus

Tail

Aplysia californica is a sea-dwelling snail that contains very large neurons. Eric Kandel studied the physical changes that occur in these neurons during Aplysia's "learning" process.

not release enough neurotransmitter to cause the motor neurons to fire. Thus, a change in the amount of neurotransmitter in nerve endings is one mechanism of learning.

INCREASING NEURAL CONNECTIONS

A change in the number of contacts between neurons is another mechanism of learning. Neuroscientists have seen such changes in several experiments. At Columbia, for example, Craig Bailey and Mary Chen have shown that as learning takes place there is an increase in the number of dendrites that the sensory neurons of *Aplysia*'s siphon sends out to make contact with the motor neuron, as well as an increase in the neurotransmitter content at synapses.

In experiments reported in 1989, Richard Thompson of the University of California and William Greenough of the University of Illinois detected similar changes in rabbits. Thompson and Greenough trained the rabbits in Pavlovian fashion, sounding a tone while blowing a gentle puff of air against the rabbits' eyes. After a while, the rabbits would blink their eyes whenever the tone was sounded. Careful studies of brain tissue in the trained animals showed increased numbers of dendrites. The researchers concluded that the cerebellum is essential for learning such conditioned responses.

Dendrite growth is especially important early in life, when the brain is still developing. Experiments have shown that if the eye of a kitten

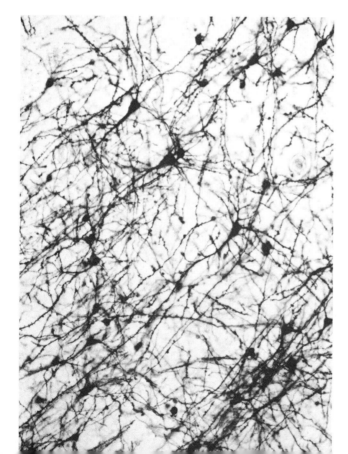

A microphotograph of neurons in the human brain, magnified 100 times. The ability of neurons to grow dendrites and make new connections even in old age makes learning possible throughout life.

is deprived of visual stimuli, the area of the brain that receives messages from that eye never develops. Anatomically, there is nothing wrong with the eye, but it remains functionally blind. The same thing can happen in a young child suffering from the condition called *amblyopia*, or "lazy eye," in which one eye cannot function as well as the other because its muscles have not developed adequately. Unless the muscle weakness is corrected early, the eye never works properly because the appropriate brain connections are never formed.

However, the ability of neurons to grow dendrites and make new connections is important all through life. It has often been assumed that mental decline is inevitable with age because the brain begins with a fixed number of neurons that can never increase and that, in fact, decreases with age. Although it is true that nerve cells in the brain die over the years and are never replaced, it is also true that the important factor in brain function is not the number of nerve cells but the number of connections between those cells. The aging brain never loses its ability to grow new connections, so learning is always possible and mental decline is not inevitable.

STORING EXPERIENCE

Many mysteries still exist about learning and memory. For example, scientists cannot yet say exactly where in the brain memories are stored. Part of the answer seems to be that they are stored in many places, depending on the type of memories—visual memories in the visual area of the cortex, and so on.

It is also clear that there are two kinds of memory, short-term and long-term. Simply remembering a telephone number may involve either kind of memory. When first given a number, a person may easily remember the digits long enough to dial them once. However, he or she may have to make a special effort, such as repeated attempts to recall the number, to put it into long-term memory.

The Cortex

The experiments of Wilder Penfield associated memory with the cortex. When Penfield stimulated regions of the temporal lobes electrically, many patients experienced memories so vivid as to be "more real than remembering." Some memories would unroll like motion pictures, scene by scene in complete detail, as long as the electrode was kept on the same point of the cortex. In most cases, the scenes that were brought back to life were not especially significant. Yet, they had been stored in vivid detail for many years.

Various parts of the cerebral cortex store different kinds of memories. Verbal memories are stored in the front part of the left temporal lobe. Visual memories are stored in the visual areas of the occipital lobe, except for complex visual patterns, which are stored in the right temporal lobe. Each person uses these memory stores in different ways. One individual may remember a list of words by seeing them in the mind's eye, another by repeating the words silently.

Scientists are still trying to discover how experiences are entered into memory. One intriguing theory has been proposed by Gerald Edelman, a biologist who won the Nobel Prize for his work in immunology. Edelman sees similarities between the immune system and the brain. Both are designed to recognize and react to new stimuli, he says. The immune system produces molecules called *antibodies* in response to an infection and stores the memory of the antibodies in specialized cells; the brain also produces memories in response to stimuli. The mechanism in the brain that corresponds to the cell that makes antibodies for the immune system, Edelman proposes, is a circuit of 50 to 10,000 neurons. He believes there are many such units, each circuit programmed from birth to form a group of nerve cells that can recognize and store a specific information signal. Some evidence for this theory comes from Vernon Mountcastle of Johns Hopkins University, who has identified more than 600 million *minicolumns* of neurons in the brain. The minicolumns are organized into larger structures for processing information. The larger structures, called *macrocolumns*, appear to be the information-processing units postulated by

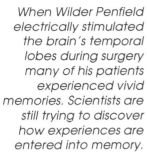

When Wilder Penfield electrically stimulated the brain's temporal lobes during surgery many of his patients experienced vivid memories. Scientists are still trying to discover how experiences are entered into memory.

Edelman. Final proof of Edelman's theory remains to be found, however.

The Hippocampus and Amygdala

Evidence suggests that the hippocampus has a role in forming long-term memories. Patients who suffer damage to the hippocampus can no longer form new long-term memories. They can remember a phone number for a few minutes but not for a day. Yet these patients retain most of their memories from the time before their hippocampus was damaged. The hippocampus thus seems to be a center where short-term memories are processed for long-term storage.

Working at the National Institute of Mental Health, Mortimer Mishkin and his colleagues examined the neuroanatomy of memory in macaque monkeys. They studied a specific kind of memory, the sort

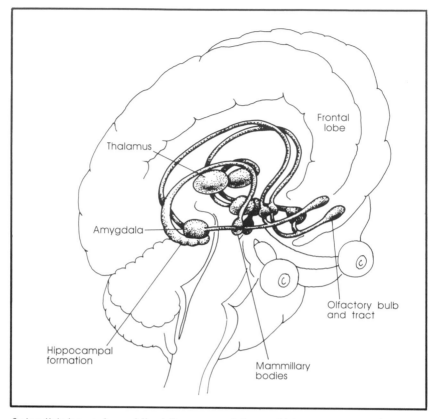

Scientists have found that the amygdala and hippocampus play important roles in memory. If these two centers are lost in both hemispheres of the brain, complete amnesia occurs.

that allows recognition of an object after it has been seen one or more times. Their research, as expected, showed that the hippocampus played a major role in this kind of memory. But another part of the brain, the amygdala, was equally important. Loss of both centers in both hemispheres of the brain led to complete *amnesia* (loss of memory). Similarly, memory is severely impaired in human patients who have suffered damage to the amygdala and the hippocampus on both sides of the brain.

The amygdala is a kind of crossroad in the brain. It has connections to all the sensory centers of the cortex and also has neurons that communicate with the thalamus and the hypothalamus. Those connections, Mishkin wrote, led him to wonder whether the amygdala "might be responsible for associating memories formed in different senses." Such associated memories are an important part of human experience: A sight, sound, or smell may bring back a whole complex memory. Probably the most noted account of this kind of memory is the story told by Marcel Proust in his work of fiction *Remembrance of Things Past*, in which the taste of a madeleine, a small cake, brings back all the memories of many years ago, an experience that starts a seven-volume reminiscence.

Mishkin and his associates found that both the amygdala and the hippocampus are involved in memory arising from a single sense, such as sight or touch; the loss of one or the other did not eliminate that ability. When researchers tested for memories that involve the association of different senses—the ability of a sight to arouse memory of an odor or of a sound to be associated with a visual scene—they found that the amygdala alone is essential.

Other Brain Centers

Further experiments indicated that other centers of the brain play roles in different aspects of memory. According to Mishkin, the brain's *corpus striatum*, a component of the complex set of structures known as the basal ganglia, seems to be involved when people learn various habits, that is, those actions they perform almost without thinking. The striatum receives signals from many parts of the cortex, and its neurons have fibers that run to parts of the brain that control motion. Thus, it provides a link between stimulus and response that leads to the formation of habitual behavior. In animal studies, damage to the striatum limits the ability to form habits.

Problems brought about by severe alcoholism offer more clues to the mechanisms behind learning and memory. Years of heavy drinking can damage both the thalamus and the hypothalamus. This can cause *Korsakoff's psychosis*, in which patients not only have severely deficient memories but also have difficulty learning anything new.

Forgetting

Solving the mysteries of learning and memory also involves discovering what happens when the mind forgets. In fact, forgetting is as essential a function as remembering. If people could forget nothing, the brain would be overwhelmed. Wilder Penfield's work showed that the brain contains many vivid memories that are somehow kept out of reach. He wrote that "it seems reasonable to suppose that the record is complete and that it really does include all periods of each individual's waking conscious life." Supporting this argument is the remarkable example of a Russian newspaperman, known only as S., whose memory was literally unlimited because he had a limited ability to forget. Psychologist A. S. Luria, who began studying S. in the 1920s, found that the man could effortlessly recall long tables of numbers or words even years after he memorized them. Indeed, S. had to devise methods of forgetting some of the facts that clogged his mind. He would write them on an imaginary blackboard and then erase them.

Most people have memories that are much more selective. Many remember important facts and can dredge up less important memories with an effort.

However, suggestion plays a role in distorting memory. Psychologist Elizabeth Loftus of the University of Washington has shown that the evidence given by eyewitnesses is oftentimes not trustworthy, because remembrance of a scene can be changed by altering the way the witness is questioned about it. Her work is another indication that scientists still have much to learn about the shaping of memory.

CHAPTER 7

ERRORS IN
THE SYSTEM

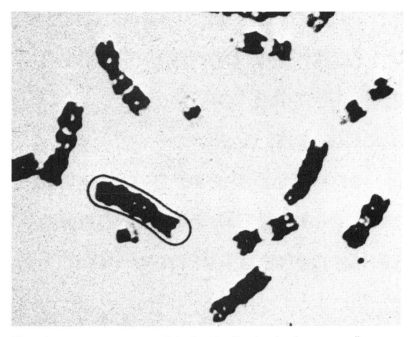

The chromosome responsible for Huntington's chorea, a disease that not only attacks movement and speech but also causes dementia

When the nervous system is impaired, the body cannot function normally. Problems present at birth, damage incurred during one's lifetime, or diseases that cause the body to slowly degenerate may cause dysfunction of the nervous system and death to the individual. As neuroscientists learn more about the nervous system, they are better able to find effective treatments for damage and disease.

HEREDITARY DISEASE

Through genetic counseling, physicians are becoming better at determining whether a hereditary disease may show up in a couple's offspring. For example, Huntington's chorea is a rare, fatal hereditary disease transmitted by an abnormal dominant gene. Victims of Huntington's suffer spasmodic movement, difficulty with speech, and psychological disorder leading to a severe loss of mental function, a condition known as *dementia*. Because the disease develops very late in life, sometimes occurring in individuals at age 50 or 60, grandchildren may have already been born with it. It is hoped, however, that if the presence of the gene can be detected earlier in an individual, this may enable him or her to make an educated decision concerning whether or not to have children. Genetic disease can also be detected after conception in the fetal stage by *amniocentesis*, and this information can allow parents to decide whether or not to continue a pregnancy.

BRAIN DAMAGE

One good way to learn about a living system is to examine what happens when things go wrong. This method of studying the human nervous system has proven fruitful to the researcher, who can look at the damage done to a specific area of the brain and relate an obvious defect in function to that area. Much of what is known about higher neural functions such as speech comes from this technique.

Aphasia

Studies of people with damage to the left side of the brain have supplied detailed information about *aphasia*, the loss of language ability. Not only have scientists learned that the left side of the brain controls language, but they can also correlate different kinds of aphasia with damage to specific parts of the left hemisphere.

In one speech syndrome, *Broca's aphasia* (named after the French pathologist), a patient's grammar becomes poor and he or she talks in short, disconnected sentences, as if reading from a telegram. The condition is associated with damage to the frontal part of the left hemisphere, known as *Broca's area*. Patients with *Wernicke's aphasia*, named after the German neurologist Carl Wernicke, talk fluent non-sense—complete sentences that only appear to be meaningful. The disease appears to be the result of damage to the rear part of the hemisphere. *Anomic aphasia*, whose sufferers can stammer endlessly while trying to find the right word for a common object, is associated with damage to the temporal parietal lobe.

Agnosia

There is a fascinating variety of brain syndromes affecting functions other than speech. Oliver Sacks, a New York neurologist, wrote a best-selling book, *The Man Who Mistook His Wife for a Hat*, which consists largely of case histories of such syndromes. The title refers to

Damage to the portion of the brain known as Broca's area cripples the victim's ability to make sense when he or she speaks.

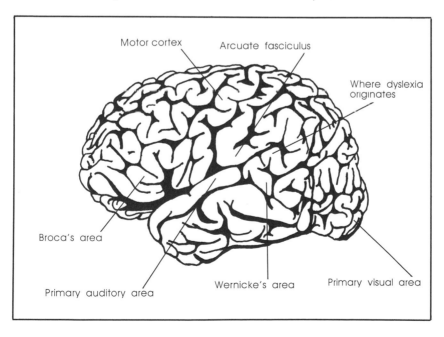

a musician with *agnosia*, a condition that left him unable to identify objects and people as anything but abstract structures; he described a rose as "a convoluted red form with a linear green attachment" and did mistake his wife for his hat.

Other curious syndromes have also been described. A condition called *prosopagnosia* leaves people unable to recognize familiar faces. Another condition prevents patients from differentiating among human-made objects; yet another causes an inability to tell one animal from another.

Apraxia

People with *apraxia* cannot perform skilled, complicated movements, even though nerve cell pathways between their brain and muscles are intact. One type of apraxia is *agraphia*, the inability to write or draw. Many of these conditions have been described only recently, and neurologists are working to relate them to specific brain centers.

DEGENERATIVE DISEASES

Some people may think of degenerative disease, especially of the brain, as symptomatic of old age. However, many diseases of the nervous system occur in young people as well as old. For example, multiple sclerosis, a disease thought to be caused by some viral agent, most often affects young adults. Multiple sclerosis results from the erosion of myelin sheaths and the formation of hard patches that disrupt the travel of nerve impulses. This can cause permanent paralysis as nerve cells of the spinal cord, brainstem, and cerebral hemispheres, as well as the optic nerve, may be affected.

Although some crippling neural disorders do occur with age, it is important to remember that not everyone will incur neural dysfunction as they grow old. In fact, the aging brain never loses its ability to learn because new connections between neurons are made throughout life. Although this process does slow down with age, mental decline is not inevitable. When it does occur, it is because of some sort of disease

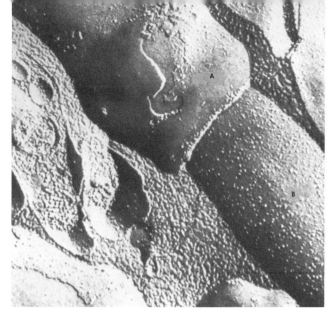

The myelin sheath (A) surrounding an axon (B) can be damaged by multiple sclerosis.

process. For example, a person can suffer a number of tiny strokes in the brain that progressively kill neurons, causing what is called *multi-infarct dementia*. The medical term *dementia* has replaced an outmoded term, *senility*, which implies that aging itself causes mental deterioration. The most common cause of dementia is a still rather mysterious condition called *Alzheimer's disease*, the incidence of which increases with age. Because Americans are living longer than ever, conditions such as Alzheimer's and *Parkinson's disease* affect millions of Americans and will affect millions more. Parkinson's disease is less common than Alzheimer's, yet it is better understood and more treatable.

Parkinson's Disease

Parkinson's disease is caused by the death of brain cells in the substantia nigra. These neurons supply the neurotransmitter *dopamine* to the *corpus striatum*, the control center for movement. When the corpus striatum runs short of dopamine, the resulting symptoms include muscle rigidity and uncontrollable tremors.

Since the 1950s, Parkinson's disease has been treated mostly with a drug called *L-dopa*, which is turned into dopamine in the brain. Until recently, L-dopa and all other drugs for Parkinson's disease could reduce the symptoms but not stop the progression of the disease. A major advance was made in 1989 when researchers reported that a new drug, *deprenyl*, could slow the degeneration of cells in the substantia nigra. The discovery of deprenyl was the result of a remarkable medical detective story.

In the early 1980s, doctors at neurology clinics in northern California began seeing young patients who were suffering from symptoms of advanced Parkinson's disease. Drs. William Langston and Ian Irwin of Stanford University traced the damage to a compound called MPTP, a contaminant of a synthetic heroin known as *1-methyl-4-phenyl-4-proprionoxypiperidine* (MPPP) made in a street laboratory. Further study found that the brain cell damage was caused not by MPTP but by a compound produced when the body metabolized MPTP. Research showed that deprenyl was one of several compounds that stopped conversion of MPTP into this damaging substance. A large-scale trial sponsored by the National Institutes of Health then showed that deprenyl slowed the rate of brain cell degeneration in newly diagnosed patients with Parkinson's disease. It is the first drug to slow nerve cell damage in any degenerative brain disease.

It is still not clear how deprenyl produces its beneficial effects in patients. The story of its discovery implies the existence of some kind of environmental toxin that acts in the same way as the compound produced from MPTP to cause the brain damage of Parkinson's disease, but such a toxin has not been identified. One exciting possibility that the deprenyl story points to is the existence of a general mechanism of nerve cell degeneration in similar conditions, including Alzheimer's disease. If there is such a mechanism, it would add to the possibility of stopping the progression of those diseases.

Alzheimer's Disease

Finding an effective drug against Alzheimer's disease is one of society's most pressing needs, because of the increasing incidence of the condition. Although Alzheimer's disease can occur in people in their early forties, its incidence rises rapidly with age. In 1989, a study sponsored by the National Institute on Aging found that Alzheimer's affected 5% of people aged 65 and nearly 50% of people aged 85 or more.

In addition, Alzheimer's disease is a much more diffuse condition than Parkinson's. Some of the brain cells that die are those in the base of the forebrain that produce the neurotransmitter acetylcholine for neurons of the cortex. Neurons in the cortex also die. Loss of these cells causes progressive deterioration of memory and reason.

When autopsied, the brain of an Alzheimer's patient is found to be shrunken and to contain *tangles* of neurons and *plaques*, abnormal formations that have large amounts of an unusual protein called *amyloid*. The cause of Alzheimer's is unknown, and there is as yet no effective treatment available for the disease. It awaits a breakthrough of the kind that has helped patients with Parkinson's disease.

One experimental treatment that holds hope for Alzheimer's patients is the use of *nerve growth factor*, a substance produced by the body that stimulates nerve cell growth. There is hope that nerve growth factor produced by genetic engineering can slow progression of Alzheimer's by preventing the death of brain cells. Studies exploring this treatment are in an early stage.

Tangles of neurons are found in the brain of patients afflicted with Alzheimer's disease.

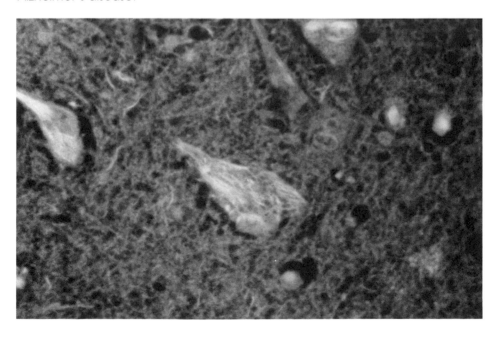

BIOCHEMICAL DISORDERS

Literally dozens of neurotransmitters have been identified in various parts of the brain. An individual neuron may put out several neurotransmitters and may respond to several, sometimes by firing, sometimes by not firing. Neuroscientists still do not fully understand all of these interactions, but what they have learned has given valuable insights into the way the brain works in disease and health.

Disturbances of the brain's chemistry have helped explain mental illness, although the explanations are far from complete. The information has come from the discovery, generally accidental, of drugs that help patients with specific disorders. Researchers have worked to determine how each of these drugs affects brain chemistry. For example, *schizophrenia* is associated with a decrease in dopamine-using neurons, whereas deficits of the neurotransmitters adrenaline and noradrenaline are found in people with *depression*. Scientific understanding of how these deficits occur and why they produce such devastating results is still far from complete. Better understanding of the chemistry of the brain is an urgent goal of neurological researchers, who hope that it can lead to better treatments for brain disorders.

REPAIR OF THE SYSTEM

Both Parkinson's and Alzheimer's diseases illustrate a striking difference between neurons in the central nervous system and peripheral nerve cells. Peripheral neurons can regenerate if damaged. Central nervous system neurons cannot. If a hand is cut off, surgeons can sew it back on and enable it to regain full function by bringing the ends of the severed axons back together. If the spinal cord is crushed, the result is paralysis; the damaged nerve cells cannot regenerate. The difference is not in the nerve cells themselves but in the cells that surround them. In the cases described above, the damage is the same: severe damage to the axon. In addition to conducting electrical impulses, the axon also transports the proteins and other molecules that are essential to normal cell maintenance. When the axon is crushed or severed, the part of the axon beyond the area of damage begins to degenerate.

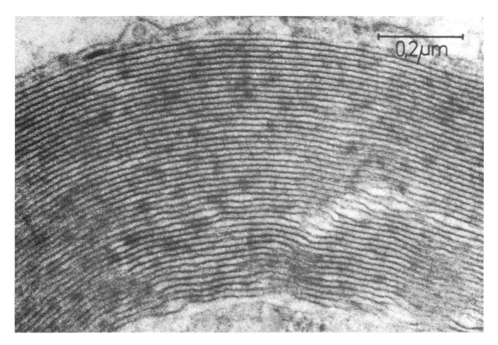

Schwann cells manufacture the myelin sheath insulating peripheral nerve cells.

In peripheral neurons, however, the axon is surrounded by Schwann cells, which manufacture the fatty myelin sheath around the axon. Schwann cells also lay down a strong but flexible sheath of tissue called the *basement membrane.* When cell damage occurs in peripheral neurons, blood cells called *macrophages* move in to clear away the debris. In addition, the basement membrane provides a framework within which the axon can regenerate, similar to the way wires force the branches of a Bonzai tree to move in one direction or another. The axon begins to grow again in a short time, eventually finding its way to its original destination.

Axons in the central nervous system receive their myelin sheaths from a different kind of support cell, the oligodendrocyte, which does not provide a basement membrane for neurons. These axons thus lack the framework to guide their regrowth. Recent studies by a German neurologist, Martin Schwab, have shown that oligodendrocytes also make a protein that inhibits the regeneration of neurons. In addition, astrocytes, cells that form a hard scar that axons can scarcely penetrate, quickly invade damaged areas of the central nervous system.

Why should the support cells of the central nervous system prevent neurons from regenerating? A major clue comes from the observation that regeneration occurs readily in less advanced species but not in higher vertebrates. One plausible explanation is that the central nervous system of higher species is so complex that the risk of faulty rewiring when an injury occurs outweighs the possible benefits of regeneration. A brain that loses part of its function is less damaging to the organism than a brain that malfunctions because of miswired neurons. Another possibility is that the mechanisms that prevent regeneration are intended to stop nerve cell growth as soon as the central nervous system is successfully wired.

Experiments by Albert Aguayo at McGill University in Montreal have shown that when neurons from the central nervous system are grown in laboratory dishes, they will regenerate if provided with the same supporting cells that surround peripheral neurons. The challenge for neuroscientists who are trying to help persons suffering from spinal cord damage is to somehow bypass the defenses set up by nature against central nervous system regeneration. Thus far, the effort is in a very early stage of development.

APPENDIX:
FOR MORE INFORMATION

The following is a list of organizations and associations in the United States and Canada that can provide further information about the nervous system and neuromuscular disease.

UNITED STATES

Alzheimer's Association
70 East Lake Street
Suite 600
Chicago, IL 60601
In IL: (800) 572-6037
Outside IL: (800) 621-0379

American Academy of Neurology
2221 University Avenue SE
Suite 335
Minneapolis, MN 55414
(612) 623-8115

American Academy of Physical
   Medicine and Rehabilitation
122 South Michigan Avenue
Suite 1300
Chicago, IL 60603-6107
(312) 922-9366

American Assciation of University
   Affiliated Programs for Persons with
   Developmental Disabilities (AAUAP)
8630 Fenton Street
Suite 410
Silver Spring, MD 20910
(301) 588-8252

American Association on Mental
   Deficiency
1719 Kalorama Road NW
Washington, DC 20009
(202) 387-1968

American Foundation for the Blind
15 West 16th Street
New York, NY 10011
(212) 620-2000

American Paralysis Association
P.O. Box 187
Short Hills, NJ 07078
In NJ: (201) 379-2690
Outside NJ: (800) 225-0292

American Parkinson Disease
   Association
60 Bay Street
Suite 401

Staten Island, NY 10301
In NY: (718) 981-8001
Outside NY: (800) 223-2732

American Speech-Language-Hearing
    Association
10801 Rockville Pike
Rockville, MD 20852
In MD: (301) 897-8682
Outside MD: (800) 638-8255

Amyotrophic Lateral Sclerosis and
    Neuromuscular Research Foundation
2351 Clay Street
Suite 416
San Francisco, CA 94115
(415) 923-3604

The Amyotrophic Lateral Sclerosis
    Association
21021 Ventura Boulevard
Woodland Hills, CA 91364
(818) 340-7500

Better Hearing Institute
Box 1840
Washington, DC 20013
(703) 642-0580
Hearing Helpline:
(800) 424-8576

Better Vision Institute
1800 North Kent Street
Suite 1210
Rosslyn, VA 22209
(703) 243-1528

Brain Research Foundation
208 South LaSalle Street
Room 1426
Chicago, IL 60604
(312) 782-4311

Department of Health and Human
    Services
Office of Information
300 Independence Avenue SW

Washington, DC 20201
(202) 619-0441

Epilepsy Foundation of America
4351 Garden City Drive
Suite 406
Landover, MD 20785
(301) 459-3700

Huntington's Disease Society of
    America
140 West 22nd Street
New York, NY 10011
(212) 242-1968

March of Dimes Birth Defects
    Foundation
1275 Mamaroneck Avenue
White Plains, NY 10605
(914) 428-7100

Muscular Dystrophy Association
810 Seventh Avenue
New York, NY 10019
(212) 586-0808

Myasthenia Gravis Foundation
61 Gramercy Park North
New York, NY 10010
(212) 533-7005

National Ataxia Foundation
600 Twelve Oaks Center
15500 Wayzata Boulevard
Wayzata, MN 55391
(612) 473-7666

National Easter Seal Society
70 East Lake Street
Suite 1500
Chicago, IL 60601
(800) 221-6827

National Eye Institute
    Information Office
Building 31
Room 6A32

9000 Rockville Pike
Bethesda, MD 20892
(301) 496-5248

National Institute for Neurological
  Disorders and Stroke (NINDS)
Building 31
Room 8A06
9000 Rockville Pike
Bethesda, MD 20892
(301) 496-5751

National Institute on Aging
Federal Building
Room 6C12
9000 Rockville Pike
Bethesda, MD 20892
(301) 496-1752

National Institutes of Health
Office of the Director
The Clinical Center
Building 10
Room 2C-146
9000 Rockville Pike
Bethesda, MD 20892
(301) 496-4114

National Multiple Sclerosis Society
205 East 42nd Street
New York, NY 10017
(212) 986-3240

National Neurofibromatosis Foundation
141 Fifth Avenue
Suite 7-S
New York, NY 10010
(212) 460-8980

National Society to Prevent Blindness
500 East Remington Road
Schaumburg, IL 60173
(708) 843-2020

National Spinal Cord Injury Association
600 West Cummings Park
Suite 2000

Woburn, MA 01801
(617) 935-2722

The Orton Dyslexia Society
724 York Road
Baltimore, MD 21204
(301) 296-0232
(800) ABC-D123

Parkinson's Disease Foundation
650 West 168th Street
New York, NY 10032
(212) 923-4700

Parkinson's Educational Program USA
3900 Birch Street
Suite 105
Newport Beach, CA 92660
In CA: (714) 250-2975
Outside CA: (800) 344-7872

Speech Foundation of America
P.O. Box 11749
Memphis, TN 38111
In TN: (901) 452-7343
Outside TN: (800) 992-9392

Spina Bifida Association of America
1700 Rockville Pike
Suite 250
Rockville, MD 20852
In MD. (301) 770-3BAA
Outside MD: (800) 621-3141

Transitional Acupuncture Institute
American City Building
Suite 100
Columbia, MD 21044
(301) 596-6006

United Cerebral Palsy
122 East 23rd Street
New York, NY 10010
(212) 677-7400

United Parkinson Foundation
360 West Superior Street

Chicago, IL 60610
(312) 664-2344

CANADA

Alzheimer Society of Canada
1320 Yonge Street
Suite 201
Toronto, Ontario
M4T 1X2
(416) 925-3552

Amyotrophic Lateral Sclerosis Society
of Canada
90 Adelaide Street East
Suite B101
Toronto, Ontario
M5C 2R4
(416) 362-0269

Association canadienne de l'ataxie
de Friedreich
Foundation Claude St. Jaques
3725 C.P. Branch B
Montreal, Quebec
H3B 3L7
(514) 321-8684

Canadian Friends of Schizophrenics
95 Barber Greene Road
Suite 309
Don Mills, Ontario
M3C 3E9
(416) 445-8204

Canadian Hearing Society
271 Spadina Road
Toronto, Ontario
M5R 2V3
(416) 964-9595

Canadian Mental Health Association
2160 Yonge Street
Third Floor
Toronto, Ontario

M4S 2Z3
(416) 484-7750

Epilepsy Canada
2099 Alexandre de Seve Road
Suite 27
Montreal, Quebec
H2L 4K8
(514) 876-7455

Huntington Society of Canada
13 Water Street North
Suite 3
P.O. Box 333
Cambridge, Ontario
N1R 5T8
(519) 622-1002

Multiple Sclerosis Society of Canada
250 Bloor Street East
Suite 820
Toronto, Ontario
M4W 3P9
(416) 922-6065

Muscular Dystrophy Association
of Canada
150 Eglinton Avenue East
Suite 400
Toronto, Ontario
M4P 1E8
(416) 488-0030

Ontario Federation for Cerebral Palsy
1020 Lawrence Avenue West
Suite 303
Toronto, Ontario
M6A 1C8
(416) 787-4595

Parkinson Foundation of Canada
55 Bloor Street West
Suite 232
Toronto, Ontario
M4W 1A5
(416) 964-1155

Spina Bifida Association of Canada
630 Wellington Crescent
Winnipeg, Manitoba
R3M 0A8
(204) 452-7580

Spinal Cord Society of Canada
P.O. Box 707
King City, Ontario

L0G 1K0
(416) 833-0984

Vancouver League for the Hard
   of Hearing
2125 West 7th Avenue
Vancouver, British Columbia
V6K 1X9
(604) 731-8010

FURTHER READING

GENERAL INFORMATION

Barr, Murray L., and John A. Kiernan. *The Human Nervous System: An Anatomical Viewpoint.* Philadelphia: Lippincott, 1988.

Bradshaw, Ralph, and Diana Schneider, eds. *Proteins of the Nervous System.* 2nd ed. New York: Raven Press, 1980.

Chapouthier, G., and J. J. Matras. *The Nervous System and How It Functions.* Cambridge, MA: Abacus Press, 1986.

Fowler, T., and R. May, eds. *Neurology.* Norwell, MA: Kluwer Academic Publishers, 1985.

Garrod, David R., and Joan D. Feldman, eds. *Development in the Nervous System.* New York: Cambridge University Press, 1982.

Gooddy, William. *Time and the Nervous System.* New York: Praeger, 1988.

Kee, Leong S. *An Introduction to the Human Nervous System.* Athens: Ohio University Press, 1987.

Landmesser, Lynn T., ed. *The Assembly of the Nervous System.* New York: Alan R. Liss, 1989.

Maletta, Gabe J., and Francis J. Pirozzolo. *The Aging Nervous System.* New York: Praeger, 1980.

Moore, Keith L., et al. *Study Guide and Review of the Nervous System.* 2nd ed. Philadelphia: Saunders, 1986.

Nathan, Peter. *The Nervous System.* 3rd ed. New York: Oxford University Press, 1988.

Noback, Charles R., and Robert J. Demarest. *The Nervous System: Introduction and Review.* New York: McGraw-Hill, 1985.

Parnavelas, John G., et al., eds. *The Making of the Nervous System.* New York: Oxford University Press, 1988.

Sarnat, Harvey B., and Martin G. Netsky. *Evolution of the Nervous System.* 2nd ed. New York: Oxford University Press, 1981.

Smith, Anthony. *The Mind.* New York: Viking Press, 1984.

Thompson, Richard F. *The Brain: An Introduction to Neuroscience.* New York: Freeman, 1985.

Wang, Michael. *Neural Function.* Boston: Little, Brown, 1987.

DISEASES/PATHOLOGY

Adams, J. Hume, et al., eds. *Greenfield's Neuropathology.* 4th ed. New York: Wiley, 1985.

Asbury, Arthur K., et al. *Diseases of the Nervous System: Clinical Neurobiology.* Philadelphia: Saunders, 1987.

Battistin, Leontino, et al. *Clinical and Biological Aspects of Peripheral Nerve Diseases.* New York: Alan R. Liss, 1983.

Berry, C. L., ed. *Neuropathology.* New York: Springer-Verlag, 1988.

Boese, A., ed. *Search for the Cause of Multiple Sclerosis and Other Chronic Diseases of the Central Nervous System.* New York: VCH Publishers, 1980.

Brain, Russel. *Brain's Diseases of the Nervous System.* 9th ed. New York: Oxford University Press, 1980.

Bruton, C. J. *The Neuropathology of Temporal Lobe Epilepsy.* New York: Oxford University Press, 1988.

Cavanaugh, J. B., ed. *Recent Advances in Neuropathology.* Vol. 3. New York: Churchill, 1986.

Davis, Richard L., and David M. Robertson. *Textbook of Neuropathology.* Baltimore: Williams & Wilkins, 1985.

De Vries, Jan. *Stress and Nervous Disorders.* North Pomfret, VT: David & Charles, 1988.

Epstein, Fred. *Disorders of the Developing Nervous System: Diagnosis and Treatment.* Cambridge, MA: Blackwell Scientific Publications, 1986.

Kryzhanovsky, G. N. *Central Nervous System Pathology: A New Approach.* New York: Plenum, 1985.

Nervous System: Neurologic and Neuromuscular Disorders. Vol. 1, pt. 2. West Caldwell, NJ: CIBA Medical Education Division, 1986.

Okazaki, Harou, and Bernard Scheithauer. *Atlas of Neuropathology.* Philadelphia: Lippincott, 1988.

Rowland, Lewis P., ed. *Human Motor Neuron Diseases.* New York: Raven Press, 1982.

LEARNING AND MEMORY

Barnes, Charles, and Peter W. Kaliuas, eds. *Sensitization of the Nervous System.* West Caldwell, NJ: Telford Press, 1988.

Caputto, R., and C. Ajmone Marsan, eds. *Neural Transmission, Learning, and Memory.* New York: Raven Press, 1983.

Matthies, H., ed. *Learning and Memory: Mechanisms of Information Storage in the Nervous System.* Elmsford, NY: Pergamon Press, 1986.

Pinsker, Harold, and William D. Willis, Jr., eds. *Information Processing in the Nervous System.* New York: Raven Press, 1980.

NEUROBIOLOGY

Conn, P. Michael, ed. *The Receptors.* Vol. 4. San Diego: Academic Press, 1986.

Jacobson, Marcus. *Developmental Neurobiology.* 2nd ed. New York: Plenum Press, 1978.

Krammer, E. B., et al., eds. *The Motorneuronal Organization of the Spinal Accessory Nuclear Complex.* New York: Springer-Verlag, 1987.

Levy, William, et al., eds. *Synaptic Modification, Neuron Selectivity and Nervous System Organization.* Hillsdale, NJ: Lawrence Erlbaum Associates, 1985.

Noback, Charles, and Robert J. Demarest. *The Human Nervous System: Basic Principles of Neurobiology.* 3rd ed. New York: McGraw-Hill, 1980.

Paxinos, George T., ed. *The Human Nervous System, Vol. 1: Forebrain and Midbrain.* San Diego: Academic Press, 1988.

———. *The Human Nervous System, Vol. 2: Hindbrain and Spinal Cord.* San Diego: Academic Press, 1988.

———. *The Human Nervous System, Vol. 3: Receptors in the Human Nervous System.* San Diego: Academic Press, 1988.

Randall, Walter C., ed. *Nervous Control of Cardiovascular Function.* New York: Oxford University Press, 1984.

NEUROCHEMISTRY

Essman, Walter B., ed. *Neurotransmitters, Receptors, and Drug Action.* Bridgeport, CT: Robert B. Luce, 1980.

Goudot-Perrot, Andree. *Electronic Chemistry of the Nervous System.* New York: Alan R. Liss, 1986.

Guillemin, Roger, et al., eds. *Neural Modulation of Immunity.* New York: Raven Press, 1985.

Hanin, Israel, ed. *Dynamics of Neurotransmitter Function.* New York: Raven Press, 1984.

Siegel, George, et al., eds. *Basic Neurochemistry: Molecular Cellular, and Medical Aspects.* 4th ed. New York: Raven Press, 1988.

Stolk, Jon M., et al., eds. *Epinephrine in the Central Nervous System.* New York: Oxford University Press, 1988.

NEUROPHYSIOLOGY

Bolis, L., et al. *Comparative Physiology of Sensory Systems.* New York: Cambridge University Press, 1984.

Brazier, Mary A. B. *A History of Neurophysiology in the 17th and 18th Centuries.* New York: Raven Press, 1984.

Guyton, Arthur C. *Basic Human Neurophysiology.* 3rd ed. Philadelphia: Saunders, 1981.

Newman, P. P. *Neurophysiology.* New York: SP Medical & Scientific Books, 1980.

PICTURE CREDITS

GLOSSARY

acetylcholine believed to be the major neurotransmitter; the blockage of the action of acetylcholine can impair the ability to retain new and recall old information

action potential a momentary change in electrical potential—as between the inside of a nerve cell and the extracellular medium—that occurs when a cell or tissue has been stimulated

acupuncture a primarily Asian technique of inserting needles into the body at specific points that are believed to correspond to various internal organs and functions; used to alleviate pain and treat illness

afferent traveling from the body to the brain

agnosia a brain syndrome that leaves sufferers unable to identify people and objects as anything but abstract forms

agraphia a type of apraxia characterized by the inability to write or draw

all-or-none response the tendency of a neuron to either fire or not fire, depending on the strength of the stimulus it receives

Alzheimer's disease a degenerative disease of the central nervous system characterized by premature mental deterioration, loss of memory, speech and gait disturbances, and apathy

ambiguous figure an image that can be seen in two different ways but is perceived by the human eye as one image or the other—never both simultaneously

amblyopia "lazy eye"; the reduction or impairment of vision, especially in one eye; occurs when the brain suppresses the messages of one eye because they are not compatible with those of the other

amnesia loss of memory

amniocentesis a test for genetic defects in an unborn child; chromosomes in fetal cells drawn from fluid inside the amnion, one of the membranes surrounding the fetus, are examined for abnormality; cannot be performed until 14 to 16 weeks into pregnancy

anomic aphasia a speech syndrome associated with damage to the temporal parietal lobe; sufferers stammer incoherently while trying to find the correct word for a common object

antibody a protein substance released into the bloodstream, designed to react chemically to a specific foreign body—a germ or another chemical—rendering it harmless; a primary molecular component of the immune system

aphasia impairment, loss, or absence of the ability to use or comprehend words; caused by damage to specific parts of the left hemisphere of the brain

apraxia a brain condition that produces an inability to perform purposeful movements, especially skilled or complex ones

autonomic nervous system the portion of the central nervous system controlling involuntary actions, such as the constriction and dilation of blood vessels; comprises the sympathetic and parasympathetic nervous systems

axon portion of the neuron branching off from the cell body and carrying impulses from the cell body to target cells

basement membrane a thin layer of delicate noncellular material underlying the epithelium, or surface cell layer, of many organs

biofeedback the conscious monitoring, using an electronic aid, of unconscious bodily functions, such as heartbeat or brain wave activity, to help patients learn to exert some control over those functions

brain waves electrical activity in the brain, detectable by electrode; can be broken down into four distinct wavelengths— alpha, beta, delta, and theta

Broca's aphasia a speech disorder caused by damage to Broca's area; marked by poor grammar and short, disconnected sentences

Broca's area area on the left side of the brain that contains the motor speech area and controls movement of the tongue, lips, and vocal cords

cell body the part of the neuron containing structures, such as the nucleus, that are common to cells

central nervous system the part of the nervous system consisting of the brain and spinal cord and not including the peripheral nervous system; supervises and coordinates activity of the entire nervous system

cerebral hemispheres the left and right sides of the brain, which are divided by the longitudinal sulcus; the left hemisphere contains areas specializing in the production and comprehension of language and is associated with orderly thinking; the right hemisphere contains areas specializing in visual perception, music, and emotions and is associated with nonverbal responses

conditioned response the ability or tendency, through training and repetition, to cause an involuntary reaction to a particular stimulus

cone retinal cell sensitive to light and color

cranial nerves Twelve pairs of nerves directly connected to the brain

dementia a class of deteriorative mental disorders involving a general loss of intellectual abilities such as memory, judgment, and abstract thinking, as well as noticeable changes in personality

dendrite a branched extension of a neuron; receives information from other neurons and transmits it in electrical form to the neuron's cell body and axon

deprenyl an antidepressant drug used in the treatment of Parkinson's disease

depression a syndrome characterized by such symptoms as decreased pleasure, slowed thinking, sadness, hopelessness, guilt, and disrupted sleeping and eating patterns; may be related to deficiencies in the neurotransmitters adrenaline and noradrenaline

dopamine a neurotransmitter produced by the adrenal gland and responsible in part for the perception of pleasure; deficits of dopamine cause the muscular rigidity, stiffness, and trembling that characterize Parkinson's disease

EEG electroencephalogram; a recording of electrical activity in the brain; electrodes attached to the head produce graphs of brain activity on a computer screen or printout

efferent traveling from the brain to the body

endocrine system a system of glands, located throughout the body, that produce hormones and secrete them directly into the bloodstream

endorphins the body's natural opiates; in addition to relieving pain, they produce a relaxed feeling of well-being

enkephalin opiatelike substance produced by the body to function as a pain killer by binding to pain receptors, thus reducing the rate at which neurons fire, which decreases the brain's perception of pain

epilepsy any of various disorders marked by disturbed electrical rhythms and spontaneous firing of neurons in the central nervous system; typically takes the form of convulsive attacks

extensor a muscle serving to extend one bone away from another

fight-or-flight reaction the body's automatic response to an emergency situation; characterized by quickness of breath, increased heart and metabolic rate, and higher blood pressure; activated by the sympathetic nervous system

flexion reflex a protective mechanism activated in response to a painful stimulus, during which the spinal cord signals flexor muscles to contract

flexors muscles that bend bones toward each other

Gestalt theory the proposal that the brain groups incoming signals from the eyes into complete images

gland a bodily structure that secretes a substance, especially one that it has extracted from the blood and altered for subsequent secretion

Golgi tendon organ a set of sensory receptors that signal the brain whenever a muscle contracts

gray matter regions of the central nervous system containing the cell bodies of neurons and of other cells

habituation a learning process during which repeated exposure to a stimulus results in a deadening of one's response to that stimulus

Huntington's chorea a rare, fatal disease of the basal ganglia caused by an abnormal dominant gene and developing later in life; characterized by severe loss of motor control, difficulty with speech, and psychological disorder

immune system a complex system of molecular and cellular components that defend the body against foreign substances and organisms

impulse the electrical message sent from one neuron to another

innate existing in, belonging to, or determined by factors present in an individual from birth

ion an atom that carries a small positive or negative electrical charge

ion channel a hole in the membrane of a neuron, designed to allow specific ions to pass in and out

Korsakoff's psychosis a condition in which memory and learning capacities are impaired as a result of damage to the thalamus and hypothalamus; often caused by heavy drinking

L-dopa a naturally occurring compound that is found in the body and is changed into dopamine in the brain; the single most effective drug available against Parkinson's disease

limbic system a group of brain structures that are concerned with emotion and memory

macrocolumns thought to be large information-processing units of the brain composed of minicolumns of neurons; their existence has not been proven

macrophage immune system cell that destroys invading cells or foreign particles by engulfing them

mantra a chant that can be used in prayer or as a part of a magic ritual and that is sometimes used in meditation

mechanoreceptors large nerve endings, located in the skin, that respond to mechanical force; differentiated from those nerve endings that respond to temperature and pain

microelectrode a minute electrode, especially one that is inserted in a living cell or tissue in order to study its electrical characteristics

mind the sum total of one's thoughts, emotions, perceptions, and memories

motor end plate the flat expansion at the end of a motor nerve fiber where the nerve fiber connects with a muscle fiber

MPPP 1-methyl-4-phenyl-4-proprionoxypiperidine; a synthetic opiate related to heroin

multi-infarct dementia a form of dementia that becomes progressively worse; it results from a series of strokes caused by hardening of the arteries in the brain

multiple sclerosis a chronic, slowly progressive disease of the central nervous system characterized by patches of hardened tissue in the brain or the spinal cord and associated especially with partial or complete paralysis and jerking muscle tremor

myelin a fatlike substance forming a sheath around the axons of certain neurons, thereby allowing the neurons to conduct electrical impulses more quickly and efficiently

nerve cell a neuron

nerve growth factor a substance that is produced by the body and that stimulates nerve cell growth; experimentation is under way to determine the possibility of using it to prevent the death of brain cells

neurology the study of the nervous system, especially of its structure, function, and diseases

neuromuscular junction the point at which motor neurons meet muscle fibers; a motor end plate makes contact with the membrane covering a muscle

neuron the basic component of the nervous system; operates by carrying electrical messages throughout the body with great speed and efficiency

neurosurgery surgery of structures belonging to the nervous system, such as the nerves, brain, or spinal cord

neurotransmitter a chemical that carries nerve signals across gaps between nerve cells or between nerve cells and muscle cells

nociceptor a nerve ending designed to perceive painful stimuli

olfactory having to do with the sense of smell

optic having to do with sight

parasympathetic nervous system one part of the autonomic nervous system that controls involuntary actions inside the body, such as the secretion of substances, the contraction of smooth muscles, and the dilation of blood vessels

Parkinson's disease a progressive neurological disease of later life that is marked by slowly spreading tremor, muscular weakness, and a peculiar way of walking

pathology the study of the nature and causes of a disease and of the changes it may produce in the body's structure and function

peripheral nervous system the outer branches of the nervous system, or that part of the nervous system that does not include the brain and spinal cord; registers physical sensations such as temperature and pain

primary nerve fiber the fastest conducting axon in the body, it signals the brain whenever a muscle movement starts or stops

proprioceptors sensory receptors in the muscles and joints; in the muscles, they detect movement; in the joints, they signal unusual strain

prosopagnosia a type of agnosia that prevents sufferers from recognizing familiar faces

Purkinje cell a type of cranial neuron able to make an unusually high number of connections with other neurons

reflex an automatic and often inborn response to a stimulus

resting potential the negative charge of a cell relative to its external environment

retina the back portion of the eye; catches images

rod retinal cell needed for night vision and motion detection

schizophrenia a mental disorder in which a person loses touch with reality; characterized by profound emotional withdrawal and bizarre behavior; often includes delusions and hallucinations

Schwann cells neurons of the peripheral nervous system, noted for their production of myelin and the basement membrane

secondary nerve fiber axon that signals the brain during the time a muscle is stretching

sensitization a type of learning that results in heightened responsiveness to a certain stimulus

spindle organ muscle bundle, containing sensory nerve endings, that is designed to keep track of the body's motion; attached to primary and secondary nerve fibers

stimulus an agent that directly influences the activity of protoplasm—the physical basis of all living things—by, for example, exciting a sensory organ or evoking a muscular contraction or glandular secretion

stretch reflex a protective mechanism, activated in response to a painful stimulus, during which the spinal cord signals extensor muscles to contract

surround inhibition mechanism used by the nervous system to help the brain pinpoint the specific location on the skin where stimulation is occurring; signals surrounding the point of stimulation are suppressed and against this silent background, signals from the stimulated point stand out better

sympathetic nervous system the part of the autonomic nervous system that governs the body's response to pain, anger, and fear

synapse the gap between the end of one neuron's axon and the next neuron, across which neurotransmitters act to pass on electrical signals

threshold potential the level of stimulation a neuron must receive before it will fire

transcendental meditation daily sessions of mental relaxation; meditators concentrate on a mantra, or short phrase, while clearing the mind of other thoughts

Wernicke's aphasia a communication disorder in which the patient speaks in fluent, complete sentences that have little or no meaning; caused by damage to Wernicke's area

white matter groups of nerve fibers in the brain and spinal cord made up of the axon of neurons

INDEX

Edward Edelson is science editor of the *New York Daily News* and past president of the National Association of Science Writers. His books include *The ABC's of Prescription Narcotics* and the textbook *Chemical Principles*. He has won awards for his writing from such groups as the American Heart Association, the American Cancer Society, the American Academy of Pediatrics, and the American Psychological Society.

Dale C. Garell, M.D., is medical director of California Children Services, Department of Health Services, County of Los Angeles. He is also associate dean for curriculum at the University of Southern California School of Medicine and clinical professor in the Department of Pediatrics & Family Medicine at the University of Southern California School of Medicine. From 1963 to 1974, he was medical director of the Division of Adolescent Medicine at Children's Hospital in Los Angeles. Dr. Garell has served as president of the Society for Adolescent Medicine, chairman of the youth committee of the American Academy of Pediatrics, and as a forum member of the White House Conference on Children (1970) and White House Conference on Youth (1971). He has also been a member of the editorial board of the *American Journal of Diseases of Children*.

C. Everett Koop, M.D., Sc.D., is former Surgeon General, deputy assistant secretary for health, and director of the Office of International Health of the U.S. Public Health Service. A pediatric surgeon with an international reputation, he was previously surgeon-in-chief of Children's Hospital of Philadelphia and professor of pediatric surgery and pediatrics at the University of Pennsylvania. Dr. Koop is the author of more than 175 articles and books on the practice of medicine. He has served as surgery editor of the *Journal of Clinical Pediatrics* and editor-in-chief of the *Journal of Pediatric Surgery*. Dr. Koop has received nine honorary degrees and numerous other awards, including the Denis Brown Gold Medal of the British Association of Paediatric Surgeons, the William E. Ladd Gold Medal of the American Academy of Pediatrics, and the Copernicus Medal of the Surgical Society of Poland. He is a chevalier of the French Legion of Honor and a member of the Royal College of Surgeons, London.